UNBURDEN

UNBURDEN
HOW TO FORGIVE & LET GO

VINCENT KOFI

This book is dedicated to all those who have experienced pain, heartbreak, and the struggle to forgive. It is for those who seek healing, understanding, and the courage to let go.

To those who have been wounded by the actions of others, may you find solace within these pages and discover the transformative power of forgiveness.

To those who have carried the weight of resentment and anger, may you find liberation as you embark on the journey of letting go.

To those who long for harmonious and thriving relationships, may this book be a guiding light, illuminating the path towards healing, growth, and renewed connection.

To all the individuals who believe in the possibility of forgiveness and the transformative potential it holds, this book is dedicated to you. May you find inspiration, guidance, and the inner strength to embark on your own personal journey of forgiveness and letting go.

May this book serve as a reminder that forgiveness is not a sign of weakness, but a courageous act of self-empowerment and liberation. May it inspire you to embrace the transformative power of forgiveness, not only in your relationships but also in your own personal growth and well-being.

This dedication is a tribute to the resilience of the human spirit and the endless capacity for healing, understanding, and love.

CONTENTS

Dear Reader,

Welcome to this book, a compassionate guide that explores the path to healing and forgiveness in our relationships. I am excited to share the insights and guidance contained in these pages with you.

Our relationships play a significant role in our lives, bringing both joy and challenges. Sometimes, we experience hurt and conflicts that require forgiveness. These moments provide opportunities for growth, understanding, and compassion.

In this book, I offer practical tools, strategies, and perspectives to support you on your journey. Drawing from research, personal experiences, and wisdom from experts, I aim to empower you to navigate forgiveness and rebuild trust, love, and harmony.

As you read, I encourage you to approach the material openly and reflect on your own experiences. This book doesn't provide quick fixes or one-size-fits-all solutions.

Instead, it serves as a guide, showing a path towards emotional freedom and healthier connections.

Throughout the book, you will find exercises, reflections, and guidance to deepen your journey of forgiveness and letting go. Each chapter builds upon the previous one, guiding you towards healing and personal growth.

Take your time, engage in self-reflection, and be patient with yourself. Remember, forgiveness is personal, and there's no right or wrong way to navigate it. Trust your own wisdom as you navigate this journey of healing and nurturing healthier connections.

I am grateful to everyone who has supported the creation of this book, from the publishing team to those who have shared their stories. I hope these words bring comfort, inspiration, and guidance on your path to forgiveness and healing.

May this book be a source of light and empowerment as you embark on your own journey of forgiveness and letting go. May it remind you of your power to heal, grow, and nurture harmonious relationships.

With earnest regards,

Vincent Kofi

This book offers a comprehensive guide to forgiveness and letting go within familial and intimate relationships. While there is no strict order in which you must read the chapters, following a suggested sequence can enhance your understanding and overall experience. Here are two approaches you can consider:

APPROACHES

1. The first approach is to read the chapters in sequential order, starting from Chapter 1 and progressing through each subsequent chapter. This method provides a structured journey, allowing you to build a solid foundation of knowledge and gradually explore deeper aspects of forgiveness and letting go.
2. Alternatively, you can choose to read the chapters selectively based on your personal needs and interests. Scan the table of contents

and identify the topics that resonate with you the most or address the specific challenges you are currently facing. You can then prioritize those chapters and delve into them first.

Guidelines for Selective Reading

- Start with the foundational chapters: Begin with Chapter 1, which introduces the concept of forgiveness and sets the stage for the subsequent chapters. Chapters 2 and 3 provide essential insights into the forgiveness process and acknowledging pain, respectively.
- Focus on specific areas of interest: If you have a particular aspect of forgiveness you want to explore, such as rebuilding trust or self-forgiveness, prioritize the chapters related to those topics.
- Revisit earlier chapters: Even if you choose to read selectively, it can still be beneficial to revisit earlier chapters later on. The information presented in earlier chapters often lays the groundwork for the more advanced concepts discussed in later chapters.

While there is flexibility in the order of reading the chapters, following a sequential or selective approach can help you gain a comprehensive understanding of forgiveness and letting go. Consider your personal needs, interests, and challenges as you navigate through the book. Remember, the ultimate goal is to embark on a transformative journey towards healing, reconciliation, and lasting harmony in your relationships.

In this book, we have included an appendix section to provide additional resources and information that can further support your journey of forgiveness and letting go within familial and intimate relationships. The appendix contains supplementary materials, exercises, recommended reading, and helpful tools that can enhance your understanding and application of the concepts discussed in the book.

1. **Reflection Exercises**: This section includes a series of reflection exercises designed to help you delve deeper into your own experiences, emotions, and thoughts. These exercises can assist you in gaining clarity, self-awareness, and a better understanding of your forgiveness process.

2. **Guided Meditations**: In this section, you will find a collection of guided meditations specifically created to support your forgiveness and letting go journey. These meditations aim to cultivate self-compassion, emotional healing, and inner peace, serving as a powerful tool for relaxation, reflection, and growth.

3. **Forgiveness Worksheets**: The forgiveness worksheets included in this appendix offer structured frameworks and prompts to guide you through the forgiveness process. These worksheets can assist you in organizing your thoughts, identifying emotions, and developing a plan for forgiveness and reconciliation.

4. **Supportive Organizations**: We have provided a list of organizations and support networks that specialize in forgiveness, relationship counseling, and emotional well-being. These organizations can offer professional guidance, therapy, and community resources to aid you in your journey of healing and rebuilding relationships.

5. **Recommended Reading**: We have compiled a list of recommended books and resources on forgiveness, personal growth, relationship dynamics, and emotional healing. These resources provide valuable insights, practical advice, and different perspectives that can enrich your journey of forgiveness and personal development.

Please feel free to refer to the appendix as you progress through the book. The resources and tools provided are intended to complement the content and provide you with additional support and guidance along your path of forgiveness and letting go.

Remember, the appendix is designed to enhance your understanding and practical application of the concepts discussed in the book. It is meant to be used as a supplementary resource, but you are encouraged to explore it at your own pace and based on your specific needs and interests.

We understand that the wounds inflicted by those closest to us can be particularly challenging to overcome, and the process of forgiveness may seem daunting. However, this guide is designed to provide you with the tools, insights, and support you need to embark on a transformative journey of forgiveness and healing.

Within the realm of familial and intimate relationships, forgiveness holds immense significance. The bonds we share with family members and partners shape our lives in profound ways, influencing our sense of belonging, emotional well-being, and overall happiness. However, these relationships can also be a source of deep pain and betrayal, making forgiveness a complex and intricate process.

In this guide, we will explore the power of forgiveness as a means to let go of past hurts and reclaim emotional freedom. We will delve into the unique dynamics and challenges that arise within familial and intimate relationships, recognizing the intricate web of emotions, history, and expectations that intertwine in these connections.

Throughout the chapters, we will address a range of topics crucial to the forgiveness journey in the context of familial and intimate relationships. From understanding the nuances of forgiveness and its healing potential to acknowledging the profound impact of pain on these relationships, we will explore the intricacies of the human experience within family dynamics and intimate partnerships.

You will discover strategies to shift perspectives, cultivate empathy, and release resentment and anger constructively. We will delve into the concept of self-forgiveness, recognizing its pivotal role in healing and rebuilding trust within these deeply personal connections. Additionally, we will explore the art of letting go, emphasizing the importance of boundaries, communication, and symbolic acts to signify the release of past wounds.

Moving forward, we will guide you in rebuilding trust, nurturing renewed connections, and sustaining forgiveness in the face of challenges. We will encourage practices of gratitude, mindfulness, and self-care as essential elements in this ongoing journey of forgiveness within familial and intimate relationships.

It is our sincere hope that this comprehensive guide will provide you with the insights, tools, and support you need to embark on a transformative path of healing, forgiveness, and personal growth. We invite you to embrace this opportunity to reclaim your emotional well-being, rebuild trust, and foster deeper connections within your familial and intimate relationships.

Remember, forgiveness is a process—a journey that requires patience, compassion, and courage. As you embark on this path, be kind to yourself, allowing for self-discovery and growth. By embracing forgiveness and letting go, you have the power to heal the wounds of the past and create a future grounded in love, understanding, and harmonious relationships.

Let us begin this transformative journey together...

WHAT'S AHEAD

Before we begin our journey, let's take a moment to look ahead at the significant steps that await us.

First, we will acknowledge the pain caused by the offense. It's important to recognize and accept the impact it has had on our lives. By acknowledging the hurt we have experienced, we can begin to process and heal.

Next, we will shift our perspectives. We will explore different viewpoints and try to see the situation from various angles. By doing so, we will gain new insights and develop empathy towards others. This understanding will help us in the process of forgiveness.

Releasing resentment and anger is another essential step. We will learn how holding onto these intense emotions can harm us. Through various techniques, we will discover healthier ways to manage and express our emotions, allowing us to let go of negativity.

Cultivating empathy and understanding is crucial in rebuilding our relationships. We will focus on building empathy towards the offender, practicing active listening, and engaging in open communication. This will help us see things from their perspective and foster a deeper connection.

Self-forgiveness and growth are integral parts of the forgiveness journey. We will learn to forgive ourselves for any mistakes or shortcomings, embracing personal growth and accepting our imperfections. This process will allow us to move forward with compassion and love.

The art of letting go will be our next focus. We will learn to detach ourselves emotionally from the past, the offense, and the offender. Through meaningful rituals or symbolic acts, we will symbolize our commitment to moving forward and releasing what no longer serves us.

Rebuilding trust in our relationships is an important step. We will establish clear boundaries, engage in healthy and compassionate communication, and learn from our experiences. This will help create a positive and understanding future, strengthening the bonds we share.

Sustaining forgiveness and letting go will require ongoing effort. We will develop strategies to maintain forgiveness, even during challenging times. Coping with triggers or relapses, practicing gratitude and mindfulness, and understanding forgiveness as a lifelong practice will contribute to our resilience and inner peace.

Throughout this journey, we will come to realize that forgiveness is a path of self-discovery, resilience, and compassion. Although it may have its challenges, it offers personal healing, growth in our relationships, and a profound sense of inner peace.

Together, let us embark on this exploration of forgiveness, guided by the insights found within these pages. May we find the strength, wisdom, and grace to navigate the intricate realms of forgiveness and create a future abundant with love, understanding, and deep connection.

First things first, let's understand forgiveness and its impact, thereof, in the next two chapters.

CHAPTER ONE

UNDERSTANDING FORGIVENESS

PRIOR TO SETTING off on the path of forgiveness, it is essential to gain a comprehensive understanding of its nature and significance. In this chapter, we will explore the concept of forgiveness in depth, shedding light on its definition, differentiating it from forgetting, debunking myths and misconceptions, and examining the psychological and emotional impact of holding onto resentment.

1.1 DEFINITION OF FORGIVENESS

Forgiveness is the act of letting go of anger, resentment, and negative feelings towards someone who has hurt us. It means choosing to release the burden of past hurts and move forward with a sense of peace.

When we forgive, we don't forget or pretend that the harm never happened. Instead, we choose to free ourselves from the negative emotions and choose understanding and compassion instead.

Forgiveness is a personal journey, and it can look different for everyone. It's not about saying that what the person did was okay, but rather finding a way to stop holding onto the pain and anger.

Psychologists study forgiveness and have identified steps like acknowledging the pain, trying to see things from the other person's perspective, and finding empathy and compassion.

In many spiritual traditions, forgiveness is seen as a way to find inner peace and heal our souls. It's about connecting with a deeper sense of love and compassion.

Forgiveness can be difficult because it means facing our emotions and dealing with the complexities of relationships. But it's not a sign of weakness; it's an act of taking care of ourselves and letting go of the weight that holds us back.

When we forgive, we give ourselves a gift. We free ourselves from the heavy burden of resentment and anger. It's not always easy, but it allows us to find healing and grow as individuals.

In simple terms, forgiveness is about letting go of anger and resentment towards someone who hurt us. It's a personal journey that brings peace and allows us to move forward. It's not about forgetting or saying everything is okay, but choosing to release the negative emotions and find understanding and compassion.

1.2 DIFFERENTIATING FORGIVENESS FROM FORGETTING

Forgiveness and forgetting are two distinct concepts, often confused with each other. While they can both be responses to past hurts, it's important to understand the differences between them.

Forgiveness means letting go of anger, resentment, and negative feelings towards someone who has hurt us. It's a conscious choice to release ourselves from the emotional burden caused by the wrongdoing. When we forgive, we acknowledge the pain but choose not to hold onto it. It doesn't mean we forget what happened or pretend it didn't matter. Rather, forgiveness is about finding a way to move forward without allowing the past to define our present.

Forgetting, on the other hand, refers to the act of no longer remembering or recalling the details of an event or hurtful experience. It involves putting the memory aside or intentionally suppressing it. Forgetting can happen naturally over time as memories fade, or it can be a deliberate effort to avoid dwelling on painful thoughts. However, forgetting does not necessarily involve resolving the emotional impact or releasing the negative emotions associated with the event.

While forgiveness and forgetting can sometimes go hand in hand, they are not interchangeable. It's possible to forgive someone without forgetting what they did. Forgiveness is a process of emotional healing and growth, whereas forgetting is more about the absence of memory.

Forgiveness allows us to find inner peace and move forward in our lives, even when we remember the hurtful event. It's a conscious decision to release ourselves from the negative emotions that hold us back. By forgiving, we open ourselves to healing, personal growth, and the possibility of rebuilding trust and healthy relationships.

Forgetting, on the other hand, may provide temporary relief from the pain associated with a hurtful event. However, it can also hinder our ability to learn from past experiences and set healthy boundaries in the future. Forgetting doesn't address the emotional impact of the event, and unresolved emotions may resurface later on.

In summary, forgiveness is about releasing anger and resentment towards someone who hurt us, while forgetting refers to no longer recalling the details of a past hurt. Forgiveness is a process of emotional healing and growth, allowing us to find peace even when we remember the hurtful event. Forgetting, on the other hand, involves the absence of memory but may not address the emotional impact or promote personal growth. It's essential to differentiate between forgiveness and forgetting to navigate our healing journeys effectively.

1.3 MYTHS AND MISCONCEPTIONS ABOUT FORGIVENESS

Forgiveness is a powerful and transformative process, but there are several myths and misconceptions surrounding it. Let's take a closer look at some of these common misunderstandings.

1. **Forgiveness means condoning or forgetting**. One myth about forgiveness is that it implies condoning the actions of the person who hurt us or forgetting what happened. In reality, forgiveness is about releasing the negative emotions and finding a way to move forward, while still acknowledging the harm that was done. It doesn't mean we have to accept or justify the wrongdoing, but rather choosing not to let it define us.

2. **Forgiveness is a sign of weakness**. Some people believe that forgiving is a sign of weakness or letting the offender off the hook. However, forgiveness requires strength and courage. It takes inner resilience to face the pain, process the emotions, and choose compassion and understanding over anger and revenge. Forgiving is an act of self-care and personal growth.

3. **Forgiveness is a one-time event**. Another misconception is that forgiveness is a one-time event or a quick fix. In reality, forgiveness is often a gradual and ongoing process. It may involve revisiting our emotions, working through layers of hurt, and continually choosing forgiveness as new challenges arise. It's a journey that unfolds over time, and it's okay if it takes longer than expected.

4. **Forgiveness requires reconciliation**. Forgiving someone does not automatically mean we have to reconcile with them or continue the same relationship. Reconciliation is a separate process that involves rebuilding trust and restoring the

connection. Forgiveness can be a personal choice that allows us to let go of negative emotions, regardless of whether reconciliation is possible or desired.

5. **Forgiveness is solely for the benefit of the offender**. Some people mistakenly believe that forgiveness is about benefiting the person who harmed us. However, forgiveness is primarily for our own well-being. By releasing the anger and resentment, we free ourselves from the burden of carrying those negative emotions. Forgiving allows us to find peace, heal our wounds, and live a more fulfilling life.

6. **Forgiveness is easy**. Forgiveness is often portrayed as a simple and easy task, but the reality is that it can be challenging and complex. It requires us to confront our emotions, face the pain, and work through the healing process. It's okay to struggle and seek support from others or professional help when needed.

In conclusion, forgiveness is often surrounded by myths and misconceptions. It's important to dispel these misunderstandings and approach forgiveness with clarity. Forgiveness is about letting go of negative emotions, not condoning or forgetting the harm. It requires strength, is a gradual process, and doesn't necessarily involve reconciliation. Forgiveness is primarily for our own well-being and can be challenging at times. By understanding the truth about forgiveness, we can embark on our healing journey with a clearer perspective.

1.4 PSYCHOLOGICAL AND EMOTIONAL IMPACT OF HOLDING ONTO RESENTMENT

Holding onto resentment can have significant psychological and emotional consequences. When we cling to feelings of anger, bitterness, and resentment towards someone who has wronged us, it affects our well-being in various ways.

One of the primary impacts of holding onto resentment is increased stress and negativity. When we constantly replay the hurtful events in our minds, it keeps us in a state of heightened anxiety, irritability, and unhappiness. The negative energy associated with resentment permeates our thoughts and emotions, impacting our overall quality of life.

Furthermore, holding onto resentment can strain our relationships with others. The walls we build between ourselves and the person we resent hinder open communication and trust. Over time, this strain can lead to feelings of isolation and loneliness, as healthy and meaningful connections become difficult to maintain.

Resentment also takes a toll on our self-perception. As we focus on the wrongs done to us, we may start internalizing negative beliefs about ourselves. Feelings of inadequacy, low self-esteem, and self-doubt can emerge, hindering personal growth and preventing us from reaching our full potential.

The impact of holding onto resentment extends beyond our emotional well-being and can have physical health consequences as well. Prolonged stress and negativity weaken our immune system and increase the risk of cardiovascular problems. The toll it takes on our physical health reinforces the importance of addressing and releasing resentment for our overall well-being.

In addition, holding onto resentment impairs our decision-making and problem-solving abilities. The cloud of resentment distorts our judgment, leading to impulsive or irrational choices. It becomes challenging to think clearly and objectively, affecting various aspects of our lives, including work, relationships, and personal growth.

Resentment keeps us stuck in the past, hindering personal growth and preventing us from moving forward in life. The energy we invest in resentful thoughts and emotions could be better utilized for self-improvement, pursuing goals, and cultivating positive experiences. Breaking free from the cycle of resentment is essential for our personal development and progress.

The cumulative effect of holding onto resentment significantly impacts our overall well-being. It weighs us down emotionally, mentally, and even physically. It robs us of joy, peace, and happiness, replacing them with bitterness and discontent. Recognizing the impact of resentment is the first step towards releasing its grip and reclaiming our emotional freedom and well-being.

In conclusion, holding onto resentment has profound psychological and emotional effects. It increases stress, strains relationships, distorts self-perception, and has negative consequences for both our mental and physical health. It impairs our decision-making, hinders personal growth, and diminishes our overall well-being. Letting go of resentment is crucial for our emotional freedom and the restoration of our well-being.

1.5 CASE STUDY: BONGO'S JOURNEY TO FORGIVENESS

Meet Bongo McFluffykins, a lively and adventurous character known for his mischievous nature. One day, during his cousin's wedding, Bongo's playful antics went awry and caused quite a commotion. A mix-up involving a cake, a dancing bear, and an unexpected encounter with a mischievous pigeon turned the joyous occasion into a chaotic mess. The fallout left Bongo's family seething with anger and frustration.

Realizing the gravity of his actions, Bongo was determined to seek forgiveness from his disgruntled family members. He embarked on a journey to understand the true meaning of forgiveness. Attending workshops and reading books on the subject, Bongo discovered the importance of empathy and understanding.

Armed with newfound knowledge, Bongo decided to approach each family member individually and listen to their grievances. He patiently listened to their frustrations, offering heartfelt apologies and taking responsibility for his actions. Bongo understood that acknowledging the pain he had caused was an essential step towards healing and reconciliation.

In his quest for forgiveness, Bongo embraced a light-hearted approach. He organized a family gathering filled with laughter and joy. With his natural talent for entertainment, Bongo put on a show full of funny skits, jokes, and amusing performances. The atmosphere lightened, and the tension began to dissipate as the family shared smiles and laughter.

During the gathering, Bongo expressed genuine remorse through heartfelt conversations with each family member. He took the time to understand their perspectives and expressed his willingness to change. Through open and honest communication, Bongo conveyed his desire to rebuild the trust he had unintentionally damaged.

As the day unfolded, Bongo's efforts paid off. Laughter became the soundtrack of forgiveness, replacing anger and resentment. Family members began to see Bongo's sincere intentions and embraced the opportunity to heal the rift caused by his antics. Hugs, forgiveness, and a renewed sense of closeness filled the room.

Bongo's journey taught us that seeking forgiveness requires sincere reflection, understanding, and a willingness to make amends. It showed us the power of humor and lightheartedness in breaking down barriers and fostering reconciliation. Bongo's story reminds us that forgiveness is a real and transformative process that can bring healing and strengthen familial bonds.

So, let Bongo's story inspire you to embark on your own journey of forgiveness. Remember that it takes courage to acknowledge mistakes, embrace understanding, and work towards rebuilding trust. With patience, empathy, and a sprinkle of lightheartedness, you too can navigate the path of forgiveness and create lasting harmony in your relationships.

1.6 CONCLUSION

Understanding forgiveness is a crucial step in our journey towards healing and personal growth. By recognizing forgiveness as a choice and embracing its transformative power, we free ourselves from the burdens of resentment and anger. We come to understand that forgiveness is not about condoning the hurtful actions, but rather about finding inner peace and reclaiming our own emotional well-being. As we continue on this path, let us carry the wisdom and insights gained from this chapter and apply them to our own lives, fostering compassion, empathy, and forgiveness in our relationships. Remember, forgiveness is a journey, and by embarking on it, we open ourselves to a world of healing, understanding, and love.

1.7 REFLECTIVE EXERCISES

Reflective Exercise 1

Take a few moments to reflect on your personal understanding of forgiveness. What does forgiveness mean to you? How do you currently perceive the act of forgiving someone who has hurt you? Write down your thoughts and feelings about forgiveness, exploring any beliefs or misconceptions you may hold. Consider how your understanding of forgiveness may have evolved after reading this chapter.

Reflective Exercise 2

Recall a specific incident or situation in which you held onto resentment or anger towards someone who has harmed you. Reflect on the psychological and emotional impact this resentment had on your well-being. What were the effects on your mental and emotional state? How did it affect your relationships and overall happiness? Write down your reflections and consider the consequences of holding onto resentment.

Reflective Exercise 3

Think about a time when you forgave someone who had wronged you. Reflect on the experience and its aftermath. How did the act of forgiveness make you feel? Did it bring you a sense of relief, peace, or freedom? How did it impact your relationship with the person you forgave? Write about your reflections and any lessons you learned from that experience.

Reflective Exercise 4

Consider any misconceptions or myths you may have held about forgiveness prior to reading this chapter. Reflect on how your understanding has shifted or expanded after learning about the true nature of forgiveness. Are there any beliefs you need to let go of or reframe? Write down these misconceptions and the new insights you have gained.

Reflective Exercise 5

Imagine a future scenario where you have fully embraced the power of forgiveness. How would your life be different? How would your relationships, emotional well-being, and overall happiness be impacted? Take some time to visualize this future and write down your reflections on the positive changes that forgiveness can bring.

Note: Remember to approach these reflective exercises with honesty and self-compassion. Feel free to journal, meditate, or engage in any other reflective practices that resonate with you. These exercises are designed to deepen your understanding of forgiveness and encourage personal growth on your journey towards emotional healing and liberation.

CHAPTER TWO

THE HEALING POWER OF FORGIVENESS

IN THIS CHAPTER, we will explore the profound healing power of forgiveness within familial and intimate relationships. By understanding the transformative effects of forgiveness, we can recognize its potential to restore emotional well-being, rebuild connections, and promote personal growth.

2.1 THE RIPPLE EFFECTS OF UNFORGIVENESS

Unforgiveness has a profound ripple effect that extends far beyond its initial impact. It creates a ripple of emotional turmoil, straining relationships, distorting self-perception, and even affecting our physical health. These ripples reach into every aspect of our lives, limiting personal growth, spreading negativity, and disrupting our inner peace.

At the core of unforgiveness lies a whirlpool of negative emotions. Anger, resentment, and bitterness churn within us, leaving us in a constant state of emotional turmoil. These emotions seep into our daily lives, affecting our mood, draining our energy, and making it challenging to find peace and joy.

The ripple effect of unforgiveness also extends to our relationships. When we hold onto grudges, trust and connection become strained. Our negative emotions color our interactions, leading to conflicts and misunderstandings. The ripples of unforgiveness distance us from the people we care about, creating barriers that hinder genuine communication and intimacy.

Moreover, unforgiveness has a way of distorting our self-perception. As we hold onto resentment, we may internalize negative beliefs and judgments about ourselves. We might see ourselves as victims or blame ourselves excessively. These distortions impact our self-worth and hinder our personal growth, preventing us from fully embracing our potential.

The impact of unforgiveness is not limited to our emotional well-being; it can affect our physical health as well. The chronic stress and negativity associated with holding onto grudges weaken our immune system and contribute to various health problems. The ripples of unforgiveness compromise our overall well-being and vitality.

Unforgiveness creates stagnant waters in our lives, limiting our personal growth and potential. It keeps us anchored in the past, preventing us from embracing new opportunities, learning from experiences, and evolving as individuals. These ripples impede our journey towards self-improvement and fulfillment, keeping us trapped in a cycle of negativity and missed opportunities.

The ripple effects of unforgiveness can also spread to those around us. When we carry grudges, it creates a negative atmosphere that affects our interactions with others. Our unresolved emotions may be projected onto them, perpetuating a cycle of negativity that impacts not only ourselves but also those we come into contact with.

Ultimately, unforgiveness disrupts our inner peace. The constant replaying of past hurts and grievances keeps us in a state of turmoil, preventing us from experiencing true serenity. The ripples of unforgiveness disturb the calm waters within us, leaving us feeling restless and disconnected from our own sense of peace and well-being.

Recognizing the ripple effects of unforgiveness is vital in understanding the profound impact it can have on our lives. It affects our emotional well-being, strains relationships, distorts self-perception, impacts our physical health, hinders personal growth, spreads negativity, and robs us of inner peace. Breaking free from these ripples requires a conscious choice to let go, heal, and cultivate forgiveness in our hearts. By doing so, we can disrupt the negative ripple effect and create a ripple of healing and peace in our lives.

2.2 RESTORING TRUST AND EMOTIONAL SAFETY THROUGH FORGIVENESS

Restoring trust and emotional safety through forgiveness is a journey of healing and renewal. When trust is broken, it creates a void that can leave us feeling vulnerable and disconnected. However, forgiveness holds the power to mend the fractures and rebuild the foundation of trust.

Let's explore the steps involved in restoring trust and emotional safety through forgiveness.

The first step on this path is acknowledging the pain that was caused by the betrayal or hurt. It's essential for both parties to express their feelings and concerns openly and honestly. By doing so, a deeper understanding of the impact of the actions can be gained, laying the groundwork for empathy and healing.

Committing to forgiveness is the next crucial step. It involves making a conscious decision to let go of resentment, anger, and the desire for revenge. This commitment sets the stage for healing and rebuilding the relationship, with both individuals actively working towards forgiveness.

Open communication is vital in rebuilding trust. It requires active listening, honest expression of needs and concerns, and the willingness to be vulnerable with one another. Creating a safe space where both individuals can openly share their thoughts and emotions fosters understanding and strengthens the connection.

Rebuilding transparency is another key aspect of restoring trust. It involves being honest, accountable, and consistent in actions and words. Reestablishing trust requires a demonstration of integrity and a commitment to follow through on commitments.

Empathy plays a significant role in restoring trust and emotional safety. Both parties must be willing to step into each other's shoes, seeking to understand the pain and impact of the betrayal or hurt. Genuine empathy creates a sense of validation, understanding, and compassion, paving the way for healing and rebuilding trust.

Setting boundaries is crucial in creating a safe environment for emotional intimacy to flourish. It involves defining what is acceptable and what is not, respecting personal boundaries, and maintaining open lines of communication regarding needs and expectations.

Sometimes seeking professional help, such as couples therapy or counseling, can provide valuable guidance and support in the process of restoring trust. A trained professional can create a safe and supportive environment for both individuals to work through their issues, learn effective communication skills, and rebuild trust.

Patience and time are essential elements of the journey. Restoring trust cannot be rushed or forced; it requires patience and understanding. Healing wounds and rebuilding trust takes time, but with persistence and a shared commitment, it is possible.

Throughout this process, it is important to reflect on the experience and learn from it. This self-reflection allows for personal growth and helps prevent similar issues from arising in the future. Each step taken on this journey is an opportunity for growth and learning.

Lastly, celebrating progress along the way is essential. Acknowledge the efforts put into healing and rebuilding the relationship. Celebrating milestones reinforces the positive changes and creates a sense of encouragement and motivation to continue the journey towards restoring trust and emotional safety.

Restoring trust and emotional safety through forgiveness requires courage, vulnerability, and commitment. It is a challenging but rewarding endeavor that can lead to a stronger, more resilient relationship. By following these steps and embracing forgiveness, individuals can pave the way for healing, renewal, and a restored sense of trust and emotional safety.

2.3 REBUILDING CONNECTION AND INTIMACY AFTER HURT:

After experiencing hurt or betrayal in a relationship, rebuilding connection and intimacy can be a challenging but transformative journey. It requires open communication, vulnerability, and a shared commitment to healing. In this step-by-step guide, we will explore practical strategies to rebuild connection and intimacy after experiencing hurt. By following these steps, you can lay the foundation for a stronger and more resilient relationship.

Step 1: Acknowledge and Validate Emotions

The first step towards rebuilding connection and intimacy is to acknowledge and validate the emotions that arise from the hurt. It is important for both individuals to recognize and accept their own feelings, as well as the emotions of their partner. Validating emotions creates a safe space for open communication and understanding.

Step 2: Create a Safe Space

Creating a safe and non-judgmental environment is crucial in rebuilding connection and intimacy. Both individuals should actively work towards establishing a space where they can express their thoughts and emotions freely. This safe space encourages open and honest communication, fostering trust and vulnerability.

Step 3: Practice Active Listening

Engaging in active listening is essential for rebuilding connection and intimacy. It involves giving full attention to your partner's words, thoughts, and emotions. Show empathy and seek to truly understand their perspective. Avoid interrupting or immediately formulating a response. Instead, focus on being present and fully hearing their experience.

Step 4: Express Needs and Expectations

Rebuilding connection requires clear communication about needs and expectations. Both individuals should openly express their needs and expectations to create a deeper understanding of each other's desires and boundaries. This step promotes a sense of mutual respect and helps establish a foundation for rebuilding trust.

Step 5: Rebuild Trust

Rebuilding trust takes time and consistent effort. It requires being reliable, following through on commitments, and being transparent in actions and words. Trust is built through consistent behavior that aligns with your partner's expectations. Rebuilding trust is essential for fostering a strong and secure connection.

Step 6: Foster Empathy and Understanding

Developing empathy is crucial in rebuilding connection and intimacy. Put yourself in your partner's shoes and seek to understand their perspective, feelings, and experiences. Cultivating empathy helps create a deeper connection and fosters understanding and compassion.

Step 7: Practice Forgiveness

Forgiveness is a key step in rebuilding connection and intimacy. It involves letting go of past resentments and choosing to move forward with an open heart. Forgiving doesn't mean forgetting, but rather releasing the negative emotions associated with the hurt. It allows for healing and the rebuilding of trust.

Step 8: Engage in Intimate Communication

Intimate communication goes beyond surface-level conversations. It involves sharing your thoughts, dreams, fears, and desires with your partner. Be vulnerable and open to truly connect on a deeper level. Intimate communication helps rebuild emotional intimacy and strengthens the bond.

Step 9: Prioritize Quality Time Together

Allocate dedicated quality time for nurturing your relationship. Engage in activities that you both enjoy, whether it's going for walks, cooking together, or simply cuddling and talking. Quality time helps foster connection and strengthens the emotional bond.

Step 10: Practice Patience and Understanding

Rebuilding connection and intimacy takes time. Be patient with each other as you navigate through the healing process. Understand that healing is not linear and setbacks may occur. Approach the journey with compassion and give yourselves the space to grow together.

Step 11: Seek Professional Help if Needed

If the hurt or the process of rebuilding connection becomes overwhelming, consider seeking professional help. Couples therapy or counseling can provide guidance and support in navigating the challenges, facilitating healing, and strengthening the relationship.

Step 12: Celebrate Progress and Growth

Acknowledge and celebrate the progress you make as a couple. Celebrate milestones, big or small, along the way. Recognize the efforts both of you have put into rebuilding the connection and intimacy. Celebrating progress reinforces the positive changes and encourages further growth.

Rebuilding connection and intimacy after experiencing hurt requires patience, understanding, and active participation from both individuals. By following these steps and committing to the healing process, you can create a stronger, more intimate relationship based on trust, communication, and mutual support. Remember, this journey takes time, but with dedication and a shared commitment, you can restore and deepen the connection with your partner.

2.4 HEALING THE WOUNDS FOR THE SAKE OF THE RELATIONSHIP AND INDIVIDUAL WELL-BEING

Forgiveness plays a crucial role in healing the wounds for the sake of the relationship and individual well-being. When we hold onto grudges, resentments, and past hurts, it creates a barrier between ourselves and our partner, preventing us from experiencing true emotional connection and inner peace.

By practicing forgiveness, we choose to let go of the negative emotions that bind us to the past. It is not about condoning or forgetting what happened, but rather freeing ourselves from the emotional weight that holds us back. Forgiveness is a conscious decision to release the anger, hurt, and resentment, allowing space for healing and growth.

In the context of a relationship, forgiveness opens the door to rebuilding trust and repairing the emotional bond. It allows us to see our partner's humanity and imperfections, recognizing that everyone makes mistakes. When we forgive, we create an opportunity for genuine understanding, empathy, and compassion.

Forgiveness also has a profound impact on our individual well-being. Holding onto grudges and resentment takes a toll on our mental and emotional health. It keeps us trapped in a cycle of negativity, affecting our overall happiness and sense of peace.

When we choose forgiveness, we experience a sense of liberation. We release the heavy burden we have been carrying, allowing ourselves to move forward with a lighter heart. It enables us to let go of the past, embrace the present, and create a more positive future.

Forgiveness promotes personal growth and inner healing. It allows us to learn from our experiences and become more resilient. Through forgiveness, we develop empathy, understanding, and a deeper sense of self-awareness.

We cultivate the capacity to respond to challenges with grace and compassion.

Moreover, forgiveness fosters a healthier and more harmonious relationship dynamic. It encourages open communication, vulnerability, and trust. As we let go of past grievances, we create space for deeper connection, intimacy, and mutual support.

However, it's important to note that forgiveness is not always easy or instantaneous. It is a process that takes time, patience, and self-reflection. It may require seeking therapy or professional guidance to navigate complex emotions and experiences.

To cultivate forgiveness, it is helpful to practice empathy and put ourselves in the other person's shoes. Trying to understand their perspective and motivations can create empathy and facilitate forgiveness. Additionally, practicing self-compassion is essential, as forgiving ourselves is often intertwined with forgiving others.

In conclusion, forgiveness has the power to heal the wounds within a relationship and promote individual well-being. It is a transformative process that liberates us from the negative emotions that hinder our growth and happiness. By embracing forgiveness, we create an environment of love, understanding, and emotional healing, allowing both the relationship and ourselves to thrive.

2.5 HOW FORGIVENESS BENEFITS THE FORGIVER

Forgiveness is not just about letting go of past hurts or reconciling with others; it also brings numerous benefits to the forgiver's life. When we choose to forgive, we open ourselves up to a multitude of positive changes that have a profound impact on our well-being and overall happiness.

First and foremost, forgiveness is a powerful tool for personal healing. When we hold onto anger, resentment, and grudges, it keeps us trapped in a cycle of negative emotions. These emotions can lead to stress, anxiety, and even physical health issues. By practicing forgiveness, we release ourselves from the emotional burden and experience a sense of relief and freedom. Letting go of past grievances allows us to heal and move forward with our lives.

Forgiveness also cultivates inner peace and emotional well-being. When we forgive, we let go of the constant rumination and replaying of hurtful events in our minds. Instead of dwelling on the past, forgiveness enables us to focus on the present moment and create a positive future. It frees up mental and emotional energy, allowing us to invest it in more fulfilling aspects of life.

Moreover, forgiveness promotes empathy and compassion within ourselves. As we learn to forgive others, we develop a deeper understanding of human fallibility and our shared experiences. This heightened empathy extends not only to others but also to ourselves. We become more forgiving and compassionate towards our own mistakes and shortcomings, fostering self-acceptance and self-love.

Forgiveness also strengthens our relationships. Holding onto grudges and harboring resentment creates barriers between ourselves and others. It hampers communication, trust, and intimacy. When we choose forgiveness, we create space for healing and rebuilding the relationship. It opens the door to genuine connection, empathy, and understanding. By forgiving others, we contribute to the creation of healthier and more harmonious relationships.

Furthermore, forgiveness promotes personal growth and resilience. It allows us to learn from our experiences, reflect on our own behaviors, and develop a greater sense of self-awareness. By recognizing the lessons learned from difficult situations, we can grow stronger and become more resilient in the face of future challenges.

Lastly, forgiveness liberates us from the role of a victim. When we hold onto grudges, we often see ourselves as victims of someone else's actions. By choosing forgiveness, we reclaim our power and take control of our own emotional well-being. We no longer allow the actions of others to define us or hold us back. Forgiveness empowers us to rise above the hurt and live a life filled with joy, love, and fulfillment.

In conclusion, forgiveness brings a multitude of benefits to the forgiver. It promotes personal healing, inner peace, empathy, and compassion. It strengthens relationships, fosters personal growth, and liberates us from the role of a victim. By embracing forgiveness, we create a life filled with happiness, resilience, and a deep sense of well-being.

2.6 FORGIVENESS AS A JOURNEY, NOT AN EVENT

Forgiveness is often perceived as a singular event, a moment where we decide to let go of past hurts and move forward. However, the reality is that forgiveness is a journey—a process that unfolds over time, requiring patience, self-reflection, and emotional growth.

Unlike an instant switch that can be turned on and off, forgiveness involves a series of steps and stages. It's important to recognize that each person's journey of forgiveness is unique, and there is no set timeline or "right" way to forgive. It's a deeply personal experience that unfolds at its own pace.

The journey of forgiveness begins with acknowledging the pain and hurt caused by someone's actions. It involves allowing ourselves to fully feel and process the emotions that arise, such as anger, sadness, or betrayal. By acknowledging and validating our emotions, we create a space for healing and understanding.

Next, forgiveness invites us to gain a deeper understanding of the circumstances surrounding the hurtful event. This stage involves reflecting on the factors that may have contributed to the situation, including the intentions, motivations, and vulnerabilities of all parties involved. It's an opportunity to cultivate empathy and see the situation from different perspectives.

Empathy plays a vital role in the journey of forgiveness. It allows us to put ourselves in the shoes of the person who hurt us, to recognize their humanity and the complexity of their own experiences. By developing empathy, we can begin to let go of the anger and resentment that may have consumed us.

However, forgiveness does not mean forgetting or condoning the actions that caused the hurt. It's important to set healthy boundaries and protect ourselves from further harm. Forgiveness is about releasing the negative emotions attached to the event while also maintaining our self-worth and personal well-being.

As the journey of forgiveness progresses, we may find ourselves experiencing moments of resistance or setbacks. It's natural to have moments of doubt or revisit the pain we thought we had already forgiven. During these times, it's essential to practice self-compassion and patience. It's okay to take a step back and give ourselves the time and space needed to heal.

The journey of forgiveness is not linear but rather cyclical. We may revisit certain emotions or stages multiple times as we continue to process and heal. Each cycle brings us closer to a place of genuine forgiveness, where we can find peace and closure.

It's important to remember that forgiveness is a personal choice, and there is no pressure to forgive until we are ready. It's a journey that requires self-reflection, inner work, and a willingness to let go of the past. It's a gift we give ourselves, freeing ourselves from the burden of resentment and opening the door to emotional freedom and healing.

Finally, forgiveness is not a one-time event but a transformative journey. It involves acknowledging our pain, understanding the circumstances, cultivating empathy, setting boundaries, and practicing self-compassion. It's a process that unfolds at its own pace, with each person's journey being unique. By embarking on the journey of forgiveness, we can find healing, inner peace, and emotional freedom.

2.7 CASE STUDY: SERAPHINA'S QUEST FOR HEALING AND FORGIVENESS

Meet Seraphina Evergreen, an extraordinary individual who embarked on a remarkable journey of healing and forgiveness. Seraphina's life took an unexpected turn when she was involved in a car accident that left her with a serious injury. As she struggled to recover physically, she soon realized that the emotional scars ran much deeper.

Recognizing the healing power of forgiveness, Seraphina delved into the exploration of her own emotions. She sought therapy and attended support groups to address the trauma and pain that lingered within her. Through these experiences, she discovered that forgiveness was not just about letting go of resentment towards others, but also about forgiving herself for any self-blame or guilt she carried.

In her quest for healing, Seraphina discovered the therapeutic benefits of creative expression. Through painting and writing, she found solace and a means to process her emotions. Seraphina's artwork and writings became a personal testament to her journey, serving as a visual reminder of her resilience and a source of inspiration for others facing their own challenges.

As Seraphina continued her healing process, she realized the power of empathy and compassion in fostering forgiveness. She engaged in acts of kindness, volunteering at a local shelter and offering support to those in need. These experiences not only helped her connect with others on a deeper level but also allowed her to see the common humanity shared by all individuals.

In her pursuit of forgiveness, Seraphina learned the importance of self-care and self-compassion. She embraced activities such as meditation and mindfulness, which helped her cultivate inner peace and acceptance. Seraphina realized that by extending forgiveness to herself, she could release the burden of past mistakes and focus on her own growth and well-being.

Through her journey, Seraphina's relationships with others began to transform. She reached out to those she had felt resentment towards and initiated open and honest conversations. She expressed her feelings, listened to their perspectives, and worked towards finding common ground. Seraphina understood that forgiveness was a two-way street, requiring both understanding and empathy from all parties involved.

Over time, Seraphina's commitment to healing and forgiveness led to a remarkable transformation. Her once burdened heart became lighter, and a sense of peace enveloped her being. The scars from the accident remained, but they no longer defined her. Seraphina emerged stronger, more compassionate, and ready to embrace life fully.

Seraphina's story is a testament to the healing power of forgiveness. It highlights the significance of self-forgiveness, creative expression, empathy, and personal growth in the journey towards healing. Seraphina's experiences remind us that forgiveness is a profound process that can bring immense healing, allowing us to move forward with renewed hope and a greater capacity for compassion.

May Seraphina's story inspire you to embark on your own journey of healing and forgiveness. Remember that it is never too late to find peace within, to extend forgiveness to others and yourself, and to embrace the transformative power of healing.

2.8 CONCLUSION

The healing power of forgiveness is immense and transformative. Through forgiveness, we release ourselves from the chains of bitterness and resentment, allowing for emotional liberation and growth. By embracing forgiveness as a process of letting go, practicing self-compassion, and cultivating empathy, we create the space for healing and restoration in our relationships. As we conclude this chapter, let us carry the understanding of forgiveness's healing potential and the tools we have learned to apply them in our own lives. By nurturing forgiveness within ourselves and extending it to others, we pave the way for deeper connections, inner peace, and a brighter future.

2.9 REFLECTIVE EXERCISE

Take a moment to reflect on a past experience where forgiveness played a significant role in your life. It could be a situation within a familial or intimate relationship where forgiveness brought about healing and positive changes. Consider how the act of forgiveness affected your emotional well-being and the overall dynamics of the relationship.

Write down your reflections on the transformative effects of forgiveness in that particular experience. How did it contribute to restoring emotional well-being for both yourself and the other person involved? Did it open doors for growth, understanding, and improved communication? Reflect on the profound impact forgiveness had on rebuilding the connection and fostering a more positive relationship.

Now, think about a current situation in your life where forgiveness may be needed. It could be a disagreement, a hurtful action, or an ongoing conflict. Reflect on the potential healing power of forgiveness in this situation. Consider the positive changes that forgiveness could bring, both for yourself and the relationship at hand.

Write about your insights and feelings regarding the transformative effects of forgiveness. How can forgiveness restore emotional well-being, promote personal growth, and rebuild connections? Reflect on the possibilities and opportunities for healing that forgiveness can provide.

As you engage in this reflection, remember to approach it with an open mind and heart. Be kind to yourself and others involved in the process of forgiveness. Recognize that forgiveness is a powerful tool for healing, and by embracing its transformative effects, you can create a positive shift in your relationships and emotional well-being.

Note: These reflective exercises are designed to deepen your understanding of the healing power of forgiveness and its transformative effects. Feel free to take your time with these reflections, journaling your thoughts and emotions. Remember that forgiveness is a personal journey, and it is important to honor your own pace and process.

CHAPTER THREE

ACKNOWLEDGING THE PAIN

IN THE PROCESS of forgiveness and letting go, it is crucial to acknowledge and face the pain caused by hurts. Acknowledgment is the first step towards healing, as it allows us to confront our emotions, understand their impact, and begin the journey of release and transformation.

3.1 UNDERSTANDING THE SIGNIFICANCE OF ACKNOWLEDGING PAIN

In the journey of forgiveness and letting go, one of the crucial steps is to acknowledge the pain caused by past hurts. It is often tempting to bury our pain deep within ourselves, hoping it will fade away with time. However, the significance of acknowledging pain cannot be overstated. It is a powerful act of self-care and an essential step towards healing and personal growth.

When we acknowledge our pain, we validate our emotions and experiences. We give ourselves permission to feel the full range of emotions associated with the hurtful event. Whether it is anger, sadness, betrayal, or disappointment, acknowledging these emotions allows us to honor our own truth. By acknowledging pain, we acknowledge our own worth and the impact the experience has had on our lives.

Acknowledging pain also helps us gain clarity about our feelings. When we push our pain aside, it tends to linger beneath the surface, affecting our thoughts, behaviors, and overall well-being. By consciously acknowledging the pain, we bring it into the light, allowing us to better understand its impact on our lives and relationships. This understanding enables us to address the root causes of our pain and take steps towards healing.

Furthermore, acknowledging pain creates an opportunity for growth and transformation. When we confront our pain, we open ourselves up to self-reflection and introspection. We can ask ourselves important questions: What are the lessons we can learn from this experience? How can we use this pain to become stronger and more resilient? By delving into our pain, we unearth valuable insights about ourselves, our values, and our boundaries. This self-awareness becomes a foundation for personal growth and positive change.

Moreover, acknowledging pain allows us to create healthier relationships with ourselves and others. When we suppress our pain, it tends to seep into our interactions, often manifesting as anger, resentment, or detachment. By acknowledging our pain, we can communicate our needs more effectively, set boundaries, and foster healthier connections. It empowers us to express our emotions in a constructive way, leading to more authentic and fulfilling relationships.

It is important to note that acknowledging pain does not mean wallowing in it indefinitely. It is a necessary step towards healing, but it should be balanced with self-compassion and self-care. It is essential to be gentle with ourselves as we navigate the emotional terrain. We may need to take breaks, seek support from loved ones or professionals, and engage in self-soothing activities to ensure our well-being.

In summary, understanding the significance of acknowledging pain is fundamental in the journey of forgiveness and letting go. By acknowledging our pain, we validate our emotions, gain clarity about our feelings, create opportunities for growth, and cultivate healthier relationships. It is an act of self-care and a stepping stone towards healing and personal transformation. Embracing our pain with compassion and courage allows us to embark on a path of emotional healing, resilience, and ultimately, finding inner peace.

3.2 CREATING A SAFE SPACE FOR EXPRESSION

In the process of acknowledging pain and embarking on the journey of forgiveness and letting go, it is vital to create a safe space for expression. This safe space allows us to openly and honestly express our emotions, thoughts, and experiences without fear of judgment or rejection. By creating such a supportive environment, we can release pent-up emotions, gain clarity, and foster healing.

Creating a safe space starts with finding someone trusted and supportive with whom we can share our feelings. It can be a close friend, a family member, or a therapist who is willing to listen without judgment. By choosing the right person, we create an atmosphere of trust and understanding, where we feel safe to be vulnerable.

However, creating a safe space doesn't always require confiding in others. We can also create a safe space for expression through personal activities. Journaling, for example, allows us to put our thoughts and emotions onto paper, providing a confidential outlet for self-reflection. Artistic expression, such as painting, drawing, or dancing, can also serve as a safe space for releasing emotions non-verbally.

In this safe space, it is important to remind ourselves that there are no right or wrong feelings. Every emotion we experience is valid and deserves to be acknowledged. Whether it is anger, sadness, confusion, or a mix of different emotions, we grant ourselves permission to feel and express without judgment.

During this process, it is crucial to practice self-compassion. We need to be kind and patient with ourselves, recognizing that healing takes time. It is common to experience a range of emotions, including discomfort, as we confront our pain. By practicing self-compassion, we offer ourselves the support and understanding we would extend to a dear friend in need.

Creating a safe space for expression also involves setting boundaries. We need to establish clear guidelines for ourselves and others on what feels safe and comfortable to share. It is important to communicate our needs and expectations, ensuring that the space remains supportive and respectful.

As we engage in this process of expression, it is helpful to remember that our emotions may fluctuate. Some days, we might feel ready to share openly, while on other days, we might need time and space for ourselves. It is essential to listen to our intuition and honor our boundaries. This self-awareness contributes to the overall safety and effectiveness of the space we create.

In conclusion, creating a safe space for expression is a vital step in the journey of acknowledging pain, forgiveness, and letting go. Whether it is confiding in a trusted person, journaling, or engaging in artistic expression, the act of sharing our feelings in a supportive environment promotes healing, clarity, and emotional well-being. By practicing self-compassion and setting boundaries, we ensure that the safe space remains a nurturing haven for our emotions. Through this process, we empower ourselves to confront our pain, release our emotions, and pave the way for transformation and inner peace.

3.3 IDENTIFYING AND LABELING EMOTIONS

In the journey of acknowledging pain and working towards forgiveness and letting go, it is crucial to identify and label our emotions. Many times, we experience a jumble of feelings that can be overwhelming and confusing. However, by taking the time to recognize and name our emotions, we gain clarity and understanding, which are essential for the healing process.

Identifying our emotions involves paying attention to the sensations and experiences within our bodies and minds. We can start by simply pausing and tuning in to our inner world. What do we feel in our bodies? Are there any physical sensations like tightness in the chest, a knot in the stomach, or a lump in the throat? These physical manifestations often provide clues to the emotions we are experiencing.

Next, we need to give a name to our emotions. This can be challenging, especially if we are not used to exploring our feelings in depth. However, by expanding our emotional vocabulary, we become more adept at expressing ourselves and understanding the nuances of our experiences.

There are several common emotions that we may encounter in the process of acknowledging pain. Some examples include anger, sadness, fear, shame, guilt, resentment, and betrayal. However, it is important to remember that emotions are unique to each individual, and we may experience a combination of different feelings.

When identifying and labeling our emotions, it is helpful to avoid judgment or criticism. Emotions are neither good nor bad; they are simply a reflection of our internal state. By accepting and acknowledging our emotions without judgment, we create a safe space for ourselves to explore and understand our emotional landscape.

Once we have identified and labeled our emotions, it becomes easier to communicate and express them effectively. We can share our feelings with trusted individuals, such as friends, family, or therapists, who can provide support and validation. By articulating our emotions, we invite understanding and empathy, which can be powerful catalysts for healing.

Furthermore, identifying and labeling our emotions allows us to track patterns and triggers. By noticing how certain situations, people, or thoughts evoke specific emotions, we gain insight into our emotional triggers. This self-awareness helps us navigate future encounters with more clarity and self-control.

It is important to note that identifying and labeling emotions is a continuous practice. Emotions can be complex and multifaceted, and they may change over time. Therefore, we should approach this process with patience and openness, allowing ourselves to explore and understand our emotions at our own pace.

In conclusion, identifying and labeling our emotions is a crucial step in the journey of acknowledging pain, forgiveness, and letting go. By paying attention to our physical sensations, expanding our emotional vocabulary, and avoiding judgment, we gain clarity and understanding. This self-awareness enables us to communicate effectively, track patterns, and navigate our emotional landscape with greater ease. Through this process, we cultivate a deeper understanding of ourselves and create a solid foundation for healing and personal growth.

3.4 ALLOWING GRIEF AND MOURNING

In the process of acknowledging pain and embarking on the path of forgiveness and letting go, it is important to give ourselves permission to experience grief and engage in the healing act of mourning. Grief is a natural response to loss, and allowing ourselves to grieve is an essential part of the healing journey.

Grief can arise from various situations, such as the end of a relationship, the betrayal of trust, the loss of a loved one, or the shattering of our expectations. It encompasses a wide range of emotions, including sadness, anger, confusion, and even relief. Allowing ourselves to acknowledge and feel these emotions is crucial for our emotional well-being.

To begin the process of allowing grief, we must first recognize and accept that it is a normal and healthy response to pain and loss. It is not a sign of weakness or vulnerability, but rather a testament to our capacity to love and form deep connections. By acknowledging this, we create space within ourselves to validate and honor our feelings.

One way to allow grief is to create dedicated time and space for mourning. This can be as simple as setting aside moments of solitude to reflect, cry, or engage in activities that provide solace. It is important to give ourselves permission to feel and express our emotions without judgment or time constraints. Grief has its own timeline, and honoring this process is essential for healing.

It is also helpful to seek support from others during this time. Sharing our grief with trusted individuals, such as friends, family, or support groups, can provide comfort and validation. Being able to talk openly about our feelings and experiences helps us feel heard and understood. Supportive companionship can help alleviate the weight of grief and provide a sense of community.

Furthermore, engaging in rituals or practices that hold personal significance can assist in the mourning process. These rituals can be as simple as creating a memorial, writing a letter, lighting a candle, or visiting a special place. Engaging in meaningful activities helps us honor our pain and find meaning in the midst of loss.

Allowing grief also means being gentle with ourselves. It is important to practice self-care and self-compassion during this time. This may involve engaging in activities that bring us joy, seeking professional help if needed, or taking breaks when the emotions become overwhelming. By nurturing ourselves, we provide the necessary support for healing and resilience.

Finally, it is important to remember that grief is not a linear process. It can be cyclical, with moments of intensity followed by periods of relative calm. It is normal to experience fluctuations in emotions and to revisit feelings of grief even after significant time has passed. Allowing ourselves to move through these cycles with patience and self-compassion is essential for our healing journey.

In conclusion, allowing grief and engaging in the act of mourning is an important step in the process of acknowledging pain, forgiveness, and letting go. By recognizing grief as a natural response to loss, creating dedicated time and space for mourning, seeking support, engaging in meaningful rituals, practicing self-care, and being gentle with ourselves, we provide the necessary conditions for healing. Allowing ourselves to grieve allows us to honor our emotions, find solace in community, and navigate the path towards forgiveness and letting go with compassion and resilience.

3.5 PRACTICING SELF-COMPASSION

In the journey of acknowledging pain, forgiveness, and letting go, practicing self-compassion is an invaluable tool for healing and personal growth. Self-compassion involves extending kindness, understanding, and acceptance towards ourselves, especially during times of difficulty or pain. It allows us to cultivate a gentle and nurturing relationship with ourselves, fostering emotional well-being and resilience.

To practice self-compassion, we must first acknowledge that we are deserving of compassion, just like any other human being. Often, we are quick to extend compassion to others but struggle to offer the same level of kindness to ourselves. However, by recognizing our shared humanity and embracing our imperfections, we create a space for self-compassion to flourish.

One way to practice self-compassion is through self-talk. Paying attention to our inner dialogue and replacing self-criticism with self-encouragement and self-compassion can have a profound impact on our well-being. Instead of berating ourselves for our mistakes or shortcomings, we can offer words of understanding and support, acknowledging that we are doing the best we can in any given moment.

Another important aspect of self-compassion is self-care. Taking care of our physical, emotional, and mental well-being is an act of self-compassion. This may involve engaging in activities that bring us joy and relaxation, setting boundaries to protect our energy, nourishing our bodies with healthy food, getting enough rest, and seeking support when needed. By prioritizing self-care, we affirm our worthiness of love and care.

Practicing self-compassion also requires cultivating mindfulness. Mindfulness involves bringing non-judgmental awareness to the present moment. By observing our thoughts and emotions without attaching judgment or criticism, we create space for self-compassion to arise. Mindfulness allows us to acknowledge our pain and struggles with kindness and curiosity, rather than judgment or avoidance.

Additionally, self-compassion involves embracing self-forgiveness. It is recognizing that we are human and prone to making mistakes. By forgiving ourselves for past actions or choices, we release the burden of guilt and shame, allowing healing to take place. Self-forgiveness is a powerful act of self-compassion that frees us from the shackles of self-judgment and enables us to move forward with greater self-acceptance.

During challenging times, it is common to compare ourselves to others, leading to feelings of inadequacy or self-doubt. However, practicing self-compassion involves embracing our unique journey and refraining from comparing ourselves to others. It is recognizing that we are on our own path, with our own strengths and challenges, and that self-acceptance and self-compassion are essential ingredients for personal growth.

In conclusion, practicing self-compassion is a vital component of the journey of acknowledging pain, forgiveness, and letting go. By extending kindness, understanding, and acceptance towards ourselves, we create an environment of emotional well-being and resilience. Through self-talk, self-care, mindfulness, self-forgiveness, and embracing our unique journey, we foster a deep sense of self-compassion that supports our healing and personal growth. May we be gentle and compassionate with ourselves as we navigate the path of forgiveness and letting go.

3.6 SEEKING SUPPORT

In the journey of acknowledging pain, forgiveness, and letting go, seeking support from others plays a crucial role in our healing process. Humans are inherently social beings, and the power of connection and support should not be underestimated. Whether it is through friends, family, support groups, or professional guidance, reaching out for support can provide immense comfort, validation, and guidance on our path to healing.

One of the key benefits of seeking support is the opportunity to share our story and be truly heard. When we confide in someone we trust, it creates a safe space for us to express our emotions, fears, and struggles. Sharing our pain with a compassionate listener can relieve the weight we carry and validate our experiences, reminding us that we are not alone.

Support also offers a different perspective. Often, when we are consumed by our own pain, it can be challenging to see beyond it. By seeking support, we invite others to provide insights, guidance, and fresh viewpoints that can broaden our understanding of our situation. They may offer advice, share their own experiences, or provide alternative ways of thinking that can help us navigate our journey more effectively.

Moreover, support provides a sense of validation and empathy. When we connect with others who have gone through similar experiences or who are willing to listen without judgment, we feel understood and accepted. This validation can help alleviate feelings of isolation and helplessness, reminding us that our pain is valid and that we are deserving of support and compassion.

It is important to choose our support network wisely. Surrounding ourselves with individuals who are trustworthy, non-judgmental, and empathetic is crucial for our healing process. Friends, family members, or support groups who can offer a safe and supportive environment can make a significant difference. Additionally, seeking professional support, such as therapy or counseling, can provide specialized guidance and expertise tailored to our specific needs.

In seeking support, it is essential to remember that we are not burdening others with our pain. People who care about us genuinely want to help and support us through difficult times. By allowing them to be there for us, we give them the opportunity to extend their love and care, fostering deeper connections and strengthening our support network.

However, it is important to acknowledge that seeking support does not mean relying solely on others for our healing. Ultimately, we are responsible for our own growth and well-being. Support serves as a valuable resource, but it is essential to combine it with personal reflection, self-care, and active engagement in the healing process.

In brief, seeking support is a vital component of the journey of acknowledging pain, forgiveness, and letting go. By reaching out to trusted individuals or professionals, we open ourselves up to the power of connection, validation, empathy, and guidance. Together, we can navigate the path to healing, knowing that we are supported, understood, and not alone in our journey.

3.7 CASE STUDY: ORION'S PATH TO ACKNOWLEDGING AND HEALING FROM PAIN

Meet Orion Moonstone, an extraordinary individual who embarked on a courageous journey of acknowledging and healing from deep emotional pain. Orion's life had been marked by a series of significant losses, including the sudden passing of his parents and the end of a long-term relationship. These experiences left him feeling overwhelmed by grief, sadness, and a sense of emptiness.

Orion's path to healing began with acknowledging and accepting his pain. He attended therapy sessions where he bravely shared his emotions and allowed himself to be vulnerable. Through the guidance of his therapist, he learned that acknowledging pain does not mean dwelling in it, but rather facing it head-on to create space for healing and growth.

As Orion delved deeper into his pain, he discovered the therapeutic power of journaling. Through writing, he was able to express his raw emotions, fears, and frustrations. Journaling provided a safe space for him to explore his thoughts, gain clarity, and gradually release the burden of his pain. It became a powerful tool in his healing process.

In his journey of acknowledging pain, Orion also found solace in connecting with others who had experienced similar struggles. He joined support groups and engaged in meaningful conversations with individuals who could empathize with his pain. Through these connections, he realized that he was not alone in his suffering and that there was a collective strength in sharing and supporting one another.

Orion's path to healing required him to confront and process his past experiences. He engaged in somatic therapy, which helped him connect with the physical sensations and emotions associated with his pain. Through somatic therapy techniques, such as breathwork and body awareness exercises, Orion gradually released the stored tension and trauma held within his body, allowing for deeper healing to take place.

As Orion continued his journey, he discovered the transformative power of self-compassion. He learned to treat himself with kindness and understanding, embracing his imperfections and offering himself love and forgiveness. By practicing self-compassion, Orion was able to create a nurturing inner environment that supported his healing process and allowed him to rebuild a sense of self-worth.

Through his dedication to acknowledging his pain, Orion experienced a profound transformation. The once overwhelming and suffocating emotions became more manageable over time. Orion discovered inner resilience and a newfound sense of purpose. His healing journey not only brought relief from pain but also opened doors to personal growth, self-discovery, and a renewed zest for life.

Orion's story serves as a testament to the importance of acknowledging and facing our pain as a vital step in the healing process. It reminds us that by bravely confronting our emotional wounds, seeking support, and practicing self-compassion, we can gradually move towards a place of healing and reclaim our joy and vitality.

May Orion's story inspire you to embark on your own path of acknowledging and healing from pain. Remember that by acknowledging your pain, seeking support, and treating yourself with compassion, you can create a solid foundation for healing and embrace a brighter future filled with hope, resilience, and emotional well-being.

3.8 CONCLUSION

Acknowledging the pain is a crucial step on the path of forgiveness and healing. By allowing ourselves to fully recognize and validate the depth of our pain, we open the door to the possibility of healing and moving forward. Through self-reflection, seeking support, and practicing self-care, we can navigate the complexities of our emotions and find solace in knowing that we are not alone in our struggles. As we conclude this chapter, let us remember that acknowledging the pain is not a sign of weakness but rather a testament to our strength and resilience. By facing our pain with courage and compassion, we lay the foundation for genuine healing and growth within ourselves and our relationships.

3.9 REFLECTIVE EXERCISE

Take a moment to reflect on a specific incident or situation in your life where you experienced significant pain or hurt. It could be a betrayal, a loss, or a deeply challenging experience. Allow yourself to fully acknowledge and feel the emotions associated with that pain.

Write down the details of the situation, describing the events, people involved, and the emotions that arose within you. Be as honest and open as possible, allowing yourself to express the depth of your pain.

Now, take a moment to explore how this pain has affected you. Reflect on the impact it has had on your emotions, thoughts, and behaviors. Consider the ways in which it may have influenced your relationships, self-perception, and overall well-being.

Next, ask yourself what lessons or insights you have gained from this experience. Are there any patterns or recurring themes that you notice? Reflect on what this pain has taught you about yourself, others, and the nature of human relationships.

In the process of acknowledging the pain, it is important to practice self-compassion. Take a moment to offer yourself kindness and understanding as you navigate through these emotions. Remind yourself that it is okay to feel pain and that acknowledging it is an important step towards healing and growth.

Finally, consider how you can begin the journey of release and transformation. Reflect on what steps you can take to let go of the pain and move forward in a positive way.

This could involve seeking support from loved ones, engaging in self-care practices, or exploring therapeutic approaches that resonate with you.

As you engage in this reflection, be gentle with yourself and honor your own unique healing process. Remember that acknowledging the pain is a courageous act that sets the foundation for healing and transformation. Allow yourself the space and time needed to navigate through this chapter of your forgiveness journey.

Note: These reflective exercises are designed to help you acknowledge and confront the pain you have experienced. It is important to approach this process with self-compassion and seek professional support if needed. Remember that healing takes time, and by acknowledging the pain, you are taking an important step towards your personal growth and well-being.

CHAPTER FOUR

SHIFTING PERSPECTIVES

In this chapter, we will explore the power of shifting perspectives as a crucial step in the forgiveness and letting go process within familial and intimate relationships. By examining the situation from different angles, practicing empathy and compassion, recognizing the humanity of the offender, and letting go of victim mentality, we open ourselves up to new insights and possibilities for healing.

4.1 EXAMINING THE SITUATION FROM DIFFERENT ANGLES

In the process of forgiveness and letting go, one crucial step is examining the situation from different angles. When we find ourselves immersed in hurt and resentment, it can be challenging to see beyond our own perspective. However, by consciously exploring alternative viewpoints, we open the door to healing, empathy, and understanding.

Examining the situation from different angles means stepping outside of our own narrative and seeking to understand the experiences and motivations of others involved. It requires us to set aside our preconceived notions and judgments, creating space for new insights to emerge. This practice is particularly relevant within familial and intimate relationships, where complexities and emotional attachments often run deep.

When we approach the situation from multiple angles, we gain a broader understanding of the dynamics at play. We begin to recognize that there may be factors we were previously unaware of or overlooked. By considering the perspectives of others involved, we develop a more complete picture of the circumstances surrounding the hurt or wrongdoing.

This process encourages empathy and compassion. As we put ourselves in the shoes of others, we start to appreciate the influences, struggles, and vulnerabilities they may have faced. It becomes easier to understand that their actions were not solely driven by a desire to cause harm but were shaped by their own life experiences and challenges. This understanding humanizes the person who caused the harm, enabling us to extend compassion towards them.

Examining the situation from different angles also helps us challenge our own assumptions and biases. It prompts us to question our own reactions and interpretations, opening the door to personal growth and self-reflection. We may realize that our perceptions were clouded by our own insecurities, past experiences, or unmet expectations. This awareness allows us to take responsibility for our own reactions and make conscious choices about how we move forward.

To examine the situation from different angles, it can be helpful to engage in open and honest communication. Seek out conversations where each person can express their feelings, thoughts, and perspectives without judgment. Listening attentively and respectfully to the experiences of others encourages a more comprehensive understanding of the situation.

Additionally, seeking the guidance of a trusted third party, such as a therapist or mediator, can provide an objective perspective and facilitate constructive dialogue. They can help navigate the complexities of the situation and offer insights that may not have been considered before.

Remember, examining the situation from different angles is not about justifying or minimizing the harm caused. It is about cultivating a deeper understanding of the underlying dynamics and the individuals involved. By embracing multiple perspectives, we create the potential for empathy, compassion, and ultimately, the path towards forgiveness and letting go.

In conclusion, examining the situation from different angles is an essential step in the forgiveness and letting go process. It allows us to broaden our understanding, cultivate empathy, and challenge our own biases. By embracing multiple perspectives, we can foster healing, empathy, and a deeper sense of connection within our familial and intimate relationships. Let us embark on this transformative journey of exploration, inviting new insights and understanding to pave the way for forgiveness and growth.

4.2 PRACTICING EMPATHY AND COMPASSION

In the expedition of forgiveness and letting go, one of the key elements that can profoundly transform our relationships is the practice of empathy and compassion. These qualities allow us to bridge the gap between ourselves and those who have caused us harm, fostering understanding, healing, and ultimately, the possibility of forgiveness.

Empathy is the ability to understand and share the feelings of another person. It requires us to step into their shoes, to imagine what it might be like to be in their position, and to genuinely connect with their emotional experiences. When we practice empathy, we open ourselves up to a deeper level of understanding and connection.

Compassion, on the other hand, goes hand in hand with empathy. It is the genuine concern for the well-being of others, especially in times of suffering or difficulty. Compassion allows us to extend kindness, support, and forgiveness, even when it may seem challenging. It involves recognizing the shared human experience of pain, vulnerability, and the capacity for growth and change.

Practicing empathy and compassion requires a willingness to let go of judgments and preconceived notions. It involves setting aside our own hurt and anger momentarily to truly listen and acknowledge the experiences of others. This can be particularly challenging in moments when emotions are intense, but it is in these moments that practicing empathy and compassion becomes all the more important.

To cultivate empathy and compassion, it is helpful to actively engage in perspective-taking exercises. These exercises involve intentionally imagining ourselves in the position of the person who caused the harm. We can reflect on their life experiences, challenges, and the factors that may have contributed to their actions. By doing so, we begin to develop a more compassionate understanding of their motivations.

Another powerful way to practice empathy and compassion is through active listening. When engaging in conversations or discussions, we can focus our attention fully on the other person, allowing them to express their feelings and thoughts without interruption or judgment. This genuine presence and attentiveness create a safe space for open communication, validating the emotions and experiences of the other person.

Additionally, self-compassion plays a vital role in practicing empathy and compassion. By cultivating self-compassion, we develop the capacity to extend the same kindness, understanding, and forgiveness to ourselves that we offer to others. This self-compassion allows us to acknowledge our own pain and vulnerability, promoting healing within ourselves and enabling us to extend empathy and compassion more freely.

Practicing empathy and compassion is not about excusing or condoning the actions that have caused us harm. It is about recognizing the shared human experience of suffering and understanding that everyone makes mistakes. Through empathy and compassion, we can create an environment where healing and growth are possible.

In conclusion, practicing empathy and compassion is an essential step in the journey of forgiveness and letting go. It allows us to cultivate understanding, bridge the gap between ourselves and others, and pave the way for healing and reconciliation. By embracing empathy and compassion, we open ourselves up to the transformative power of forgiveness and create the potential for deeper connection within our familial and intimate relationships. Let us embark on this path of empathy and compassion, fostering understanding and healing for the benefit of ourselves and those around us.

4.3 RECOGNIZING THE HUMANITY OF THE OFFENDER

In the journey of forgiveness and letting go, it is crucial to recognize the humanity of the offender. When we acknowledge that even those who have hurt us are complex individuals with their own struggles, vulnerabilities, and capacity for growth, we open ourselves up to a deeper understanding and the possibility of forgiveness.

It can be challenging to see the humanity of the person who has caused us pain. Our natural response may be to dehumanize them, to label them as "the enemy" or "the villain." However, this mindset perpetuates a cycle of hurt and prevents us from finding common ground and healing.

Recognizing the humanity of the offender does not mean condoning or excusing their actions. It means acknowledging that they, like all of us, are imperfect beings who make mistakes. By acknowledging their humanity, we begin to see them as more than just the harm they have caused. We see the complexities of their life, their own experiences of pain, and the factors that may have influenced their actions.

To recognize the humanity of the offender, we can start by challenging our own assumptions and judgments. We can try to put ourselves in their shoes and imagine the circumstances that led them to behave the way they did. This exercise helps us cultivate empathy and compassion, allowing us to see them as multifaceted individuals with their own struggles and vulnerabilities.

Another helpful practice is to engage in open and honest communication. By having conversations with the offender, we can gain insights into their motivations, remorse, or personal growth. These conversations create an opportunity for both parties to express their feelings, share perspectives, and work towards understanding and reconciliation.

Additionally, it is essential to separate the person from their actions. While we may strongly disagree with or condemn their behavior, it is important to remember that their actions do not define their entire being. They are capable of change and growth, just as we are. Recognizing their humanity allows us to see the potential for transformation and healing, both for ourselves and for them.

By recognizing the humanity of the offender, we break free from the cycle of resentment and bitterness. We open ourselves up to the possibility of forgiveness and reconciliation, fostering an environment where healing can occur. It is a powerful act of reclaiming our own emotional well-being and taking control of our own narrative.

In conclusion, recognizing the humanity of the offender is an integral part of the forgiveness and letting go process. It helps us move beyond the labels and judgments, allowing us to see them as complex individuals with their own struggles and capacity for growth. By recognizing their humanity, we create space for understanding, empathy, and the potential for forgiveness. Let us embrace this mindset as we embark on the journey of healing and transformation.

4.4 LETTING GO OF VICTIM MENTALITY

In the process of forgiveness and letting go, it is crucial to let go of victim mentality. Holding onto the identity of a victim can keep us trapped in a cycle of pain and resentment, hindering our ability to heal and move forward. By shifting our perspective and reclaiming our personal power, we can empower ourselves in the forgiveness journey.

Victim mentality is characterized by a mindset that perceives oneself as helpless, powerless, and at the mercy of others' actions. It often stems from past traumas or hurts, where we may have genuinely been victimized. However, holding onto this victim identity can become a barrier to our own growth and healing.

To let go of victim mentality, we must first recognize that we have the power to define our own narrative. While we cannot change the past or control the actions of others, we have the ability to choose how we respond to the circumstances and how we shape our future. Shifting our focus from what happened to us towards our own personal growth and resilience is a crucial step.

One effective strategy is reframing our experiences. Instead of seeing ourselves solely as victims, we can acknowledge the adversity we have faced while also recognizing our inner strength and resilience. By reframing our narrative, we empower ourselves to become survivors and thrivers, rather than remaining stuck in a victim role.

Another important aspect of letting go of victim mentality is taking responsibility for our own healing and well-being. While others may have caused us harm, it is up to us to seek the support, resources, and tools necessary to heal and move forward. By actively engaging in self-care, therapy, or other healing modalities, we reclaim our power and prioritize our own well-being.

Letting go of victim mentality also involves releasing the need for revenge or holding onto resentment. While it is natural to feel anger or resentment towards those who have hurt us, holding onto these negative emotions only prolongs our suffering. By practicing forgiveness, we free ourselves from the emotional burden and create space for healing and growth.

Additionally, cultivating a mindset of gratitude and resilience can greatly contribute to letting go of victim mentality. Focusing on the positive aspects of our lives, acknowledging our strengths, and finding gratitude in the midst of adversity helps us shift our perspective and see the possibilities for growth and transformation.

In conclusion, letting go of victim mentality is a powerful step in the forgiveness and letting go process. By shifting our perspective, reframing our experiences, and taking responsibility for our healing, we empower ourselves to rise above the role of a victim. By doing so, we reclaim our personal power, cultivate resilience, and create a pathway towards healing and personal growth. Let us embrace this mindset as we embark on the journey of forgiveness and self-empowerment.

4.5 CASE STUDY: KESHI'S PATH TO HEALING: ACKNOWLEDGING AND OVERCOMING EMOTIONAL PAIN

In the bustling city of Bloomville, Keshi Patel, a remarkable individual with an indomitable spirit, embarked on a profound journey of acknowledging and healing from deep emotional pain. Throughout her life, Keshi had faced a series of challenging experiences that left lasting scars on her heart and soul. However, she refused to let her pain define her, and with unwavering determination, she set out on a transformative path to confront her emotions and find healing.

Keshi's journey began with a moment of clarity when she realized that she could no longer ignore the weight of her pain. She made a courageous decision to confront her emotions head-on and acknowledge the profound impact they had on her life. With the guidance of a compassionate therapist, Keshi delved into the depths of her past, unraveled the layers of her pain, and began the process of healing.

One of the pivotal tools that aided Keshi in acknowledging her pain was the power of self-reflection. Through introspection and deep contemplation, she confronted the memories, traumas, and unresolved emotions that had haunted her for years. By allowing herself to explore the depths of her pain, she gradually gained a better understanding of its roots and the ways in which it had influenced her thoughts, beliefs, and behaviors.

As Keshi embarked on her journey of acknowledging the pain, she discovered the healing potential of self-expression. She turned to creative outlets, such as painting and writing, as a means to give voice to her emotions. Through vibrant brushstrokes and heartfelt words, she found solace and release. Art became her sanctuary, allowing her to process her pain and transform it into something beautiful.

In her pursuit of healing, Keshi also recognized the importance of seeking support from loved ones. She confided in her closest friends and family, who offered a compassionate ear, understanding, and unwavering support. Their presence provided a safe space for Keshi to openly share her pain, fears, and vulnerabilities, fostering a sense of connection and validation that played a vital role in her healing journey.

Furthermore, Keshi embraced various holistic practices to nurture her overall well-being. She explored the healing powers of meditation, engaging in daily mindfulness exercises to cultivate inner peace and calm. By focusing her attention on the present moment, she learned to observe her emotions without judgment, allowing them to rise and fall like passing waves.

Throughout her journey, Keshi came to understand that healing is not a linear process. There were moments of setbacks and challenges when her pain resurfaced unexpectedly. However, she approached these instances with patience and self-compassion, reminding herself that healing takes time and that relapses are a natural part of the journey. Keshi persevered, knowing that every step forward, no matter how small, brought her closer to reclaiming her joy and finding lasting healing.

Today, Keshi stands as a beacon of hope and resilience. Through her unwavering commitment to acknowledging and overcoming her pain, she has not only found healing but also discovered a profound sense of empowerment and self-discovery. Her journey serves as a testament to the transformative power of acknowledging our pain and taking proactive steps towards healing.

Keshi's story inspires us to embark on our own paths of acknowledging and healing from emotional pain. It reminds us that no matter how deep our wounds may be, we have the strength within us to confront our pain, seek support, and cultivate the resilience needed to emerge stronger and more vibrant than ever before.

May Keshi's journey serve as a guiding light, encouraging us all to embrace our emotions, acknowledge our pain, and embark on a transformative path toward healing, self-discovery, and a life filled with joy, authenticity, and inner peace.

4.6 CONCLUSION

Shifting perspectives holds immense power in the forgiveness and letting go process within familial and intimate relationships. By exploring different angles, practicing empathy and compassion, recognizing the humanity of the offender, and letting go of victim mentality, we open ourselves up to new insights and possibilities for healing. Shifting perspectives allows us to break free from the confines of resentment and anger, enabling us to see situations and individuals in a new light. By embracing this transformative practice, we create space for understanding, growth, and ultimately, the potential for forgiveness and reconciliation. As we conclude this chapter, let us embrace the power of shifting perspectives as a catalyst for profound change and healing in our relationships.

4.7 REFLECTIVE EXERCISE

Take a moment to reflect on a specific situation or relationship where you have experienced difficulty in forgiving and letting go. Consider the perspective you have held about the offender and the situation up until now.

Now, challenge yourself to shift your perspective. Imagine stepping into the shoes of the offender and seeing the situation from their point of view. Consider their background, experiences, and emotions that may have contributed to their actions.

Write down your reflections on this new perspective. How does it change your understanding of the situation?

Does it evoke any empathy or compassion towards the offender? Are there any new insights or realizations that emerge from this shift in perspective?

Next, reflect on your own role in the situation. Are there any aspects where you may have contributed or played a part? How does this awareness impact your perspective and understanding of the forgiveness process?

Consider the impact of holding onto a victim mentality. Reflect on any ways in which you may have identified as a victim in this situation and how it has affected your ability to forgive. Explore alternative perspectives that empower you and promote healing and growth.

Finally, think about how you can integrate these new perspectives into your forgiveness journey. Are there any actions or changes in mindset that you can take to foster empathy, compassion, and a greater understanding of the humanity of the offender?

As you engage in this reflection, be open to the possibilities that arise from shifting your perspectives. Remember that forgiveness is a complex and personal process, and by exploring different viewpoints, you are expanding your capacity for healing and letting go.

Note: These reflective exercises are intended to support your exploration of shifting perspectives in the forgiveness process. It is important to approach this process with self-care and seek professional guidance if needed. Remember to be patient with yourself as you navigate through different perspectives, and honor your own unique journey of forgiveness and letting go.

CHAPTER FIVE

RELEASING RESENTMENT AND ANGER

IN THIS CHAPTER, we will delve into the significance of releasing resentment and anger as an integral part of the forgiveness and letting go process. We will explore the destructive impact of holding onto these emotions, learn effective techniques for managing and releasing them, discover healthy outlets for channeling our emotions, and understand the transformative power of forgiveness in breaking the cycle of hurt and finding emotional liberation.

5.1 UNDERSTANDING THE DESTRUCTIVE NATURE OF RESENTMENT

Resentment is a powerful emotion that can cause significant harm to ourselves and our relationships. It is important to recognize and understand the destructive nature of resentment in order to begin the process of releasing it.

Resentment is like a poison that slowly eats away at our well-being. When we hold onto past grievances and harbor feelings of bitterness and anger, we are essentially carrying a heavy burden within us. This burden not only affects our mental and emotional state but also seeps into our interactions with others.

One of the most damaging aspects of resentment is that it keeps us trapped in the past. We constantly replay the hurtful events, allowing them to consume our thoughts and emotions. This obsession with the past prevents us from moving forward and finding true peace and happiness in the present.

Resentment also breeds negativity. When we hold onto resentment, it colors our perception of the world around us. We may become cynical, distrusting, and constantly on guard. This negativity not only affects our own well-being but also taints our relationships with others. It becomes difficult to form deep connections and maintain healthy interactions when we are constantly holding onto resentment.

Moreover, resentment can manifest in various physical and emotional symptoms. It can lead to increased stress levels, sleep disturbances, and even impact our overall physical health. Emotionally, it can contribute to feelings of anxiety, depression, and a general sense of unhappiness.

Recognizing the destructive nature of resentment is the first step towards freeing ourselves from its grip. It requires acknowledging the toll it takes on our mental, emotional, and physical well-being. By understanding that holding onto resentment only perpetuates our own suffering, we can begin to cultivate a willingness to let go.

In the journey of forgiveness and letting go, it is essential to confront and address the destructive nature of resentment. By doing so, we open ourselves up to the possibility of healing and liberation. Letting go of resentment allows us to break free from the chains of the past and embrace a future filled with peace, happiness, and healthier relationships.

Remember, forgiveness is not about excusing or forgetting the pain that was inflicted upon us. It is about freeing ourselves from the burden of resentment and reclaiming our power to live a more fulfilled and joyful life.

5.2 TECHNIQUES FOR MANAGING ANGER AND RESENTMENT

Anger and resentment can have a detrimental impact on our well-being and relationships. To prevent these emotions from causing further harm, it's important to learn effective techniques for managing them. Here are some simple strategies to help you handle anger and resentment in a healthy way:

First, develop self-awareness by recognizing the signs of anger and resentment in your body and mind. Take note of the triggers and thought patterns that fuel these emotions. By being aware, you can better address them.

When anger or resentment arises, take a pause and focus on your breathing. Deep breaths can calm your nervous system and provide temporary relief. This gives you a chance to respond more thoughtfully, rather than reacting impulsively.

Find healthy outlets to express your emotions. Engage in physical activities like exercise or sports to release built-up energy. Consider journaling or talking to a trusted friend or therapist to process your feelings. Avoid suppressing them, as it can lead to more emotional turmoil.

Practice empathy and understanding by putting yourself in the other person's shoes. Consider their perspective and the circumstances that may have influenced their actions. Empathy doesn't mean condoning their behavior, but it helps reduce the intensity of your anger and resentment.

Challenge negative thoughts associated with the situation. Replace them with more positive and realistic thoughts. Reframing your perspective allows you to see the situation in a balanced light, which can lessen the intensity of your emotions.

Engage in forgiveness exercises to promote healing and release resentment. This may involve writing a forgiveness letter (even if it's not sent), visualizing letting go of resentment, or seeking guidance from a therapist experienced in forgiveness work.

Take care of yourself through self-care practices. Prioritize activities that bring you joy and relaxation. Get enough sleep, eat nourishing food, and engage in activities that support your well-being. When you prioritize self-care, you'll be better equipped to manage anger and resentment.

Remember, managing anger and resentment is an ongoing process that requires patience and self-compassion. By incorporating these techniques into your life, you can develop healthier coping mechanisms and cultivate emotional well-being as you journey toward forgiveness and letting go.

5.3 FINDING HEALTHY WAYS TO CHANNEL EMOTIONS

When we experience anger and resentment, it's important to find constructive and healthy ways to deal with these emotions. Redirecting our energy into positive outlets can prevent these feelings from causing further harm and promote our emotional well-being. Here are some simple strategies to help you find healthy ways to channel your emotions.

Engaging in physical activities is a powerful way to release pent-up emotions. Whether it's going for a run, practicing yoga, or participating in a team sport, physical exercise can help you channel your anger and resentment into something productive. It not only provides an outlet for your emotions but also promotes overall well-being.

Practicing mindfulness and meditation techniques can help you cultivate a sense of calm and inner peace. When you notice anger or resentment arising, take a few moments to focus on your breath and observe your emotions without judgment. This practice can help you gain clarity and respond to situations with greater composure.

Expressing yourself through creative outlets can be a therapeutic way to channel your emotions. Whether it's painting, writing, playing a musical instrument, or dancing, find a creative outlet that resonates with you. Allow yourself to freely express your feelings and emotions through your chosen medium.

Seeking support through counseling or therapy can provide guidance and help you develop healthy coping mechanisms. A trained therapist can offer a safe space for you to express your feelings and explore the underlying causes of your anger and resentment.

Practicing self-care is crucial when dealing with intense emotions. Take time for activities that bring you joy and relaxation, such as taking a warm bath, reading a book, listening to music, or spending time in nature. Engaging in self-care practices nurtures your well-being and helps you recharge emotionally.

Engaging in acts of kindness can shift your focus from anger and resentment to a more positive and constructive mindset. Look for opportunities to make a positive impact on someone else's life, whether through volunteer work, random acts of kindness, or supporting a friend in need.

Remember, finding healthy ways to channel your emotions is a personal journey. Experiment with different strategies and discover what works best for you. By actively seeking positive outlets for your anger and resentment, you can transform these emotions into opportunities for personal growth and healing.

5.4 THE ROLE OF FORGIVENESS IN BREAKING THE CYCLE OF HURT

In the journey of forgiveness and letting go, one of the most powerful aspects is its ability to break the cycle of hurt within familial and intimate relationships. When we hold onto anger, resentment, and grudges, we unknowingly perpetuate a cycle of pain that affects not only ourselves but also those around us. However, by embracing forgiveness, we can interrupt this destructive cycle and create a pathway towards healing and reconciliation. Let's explore the key ways in which forgiveness plays a crucial role in breaking this cycle.

One of the first ways forgiveness breaks the cycle of hurt is by allowing us to let go of emotional baggage. When we hold onto past hurts, we carry the weight of anger and resentment with us, hindering our own emotional well-being. By choosing forgiveness, we release this burden, freeing ourselves to move forward with greater clarity and inner peace.

Another significant impact of forgiveness is breaking the cycle of retaliation. When we hold grudges, it's natural to want to seek revenge or engage in harmful behaviors towards the person who hurt us. However, forgiveness interrupts this cycle by choosing compassion and understanding over perpetuating the hurt. It empowers us to break free from the cycle of negative actions and reactions, paving the way for more positive and constructive interactions.

Moreover, forgiveness cultivates empathy and compassion within us. It helps us see the humanity in others, recognizing that people make mistakes and carry their own pain. By developing empathy, we foster a deeper sense of connection and understanding, creating a fertile ground for healing and reconciliation to take place.

Restoring trust and rebuilding relationships is another crucial outcome of forgiveness. When we choose forgiveness, we open the door for rebuilding trust and repairing damaged relationships. It creates an opportunity for open communication, understanding, and growth, fostering a healthier and more resilient bond between individuals.

Furthermore, forgiveness liberates us from the grips of negativity. Holding onto resentment and anger consumes our energy and keeps us trapped in a cycle of negative emotions. By choosing forgiveness, we break free from this cycle and allow ourselves to embrace a more positive outlook on life. It leads to greater inner peace, emotional well-being, and an overall sense of lightness.

Beyond its immediate impact, forgiveness also promotes personal growth. It challenges us to confront our own vulnerabilities, biases, and limitations. Through the process of forgiveness, we learn valuable lessons, develop resilience, and become more compassionate individuals. It is a transformative journey that not only heals the wounds but also allows us to grow into better versions of ourselves.

Finally, forgiveness enhances our overall well-being. By choosing forgiveness, we prioritize our own mental, emotional, and even physical health. It reduces stress, improves our emotional well-being, and contributes to a greater sense of happiness and fulfillment in life. It is an act of self-care and self-love that has far-reaching benefits.

In conclusion, forgiveness has the remarkable power to break the cycle of hurt within familial and intimate relationships. It enables us to let go of emotional baggage, break the cycle of retaliation, cultivate empathy and compassion, restore trust and rebuild relationships, liberate ourselves from negativity, promote personal growth, and enhance our overall well-being. Through forgiveness, we embark on a journey of healing, growth, and emotional liberation, creating a brighter and more harmonious future for ourselves and those around us.

5.5 CASE STUDY: THE JOURNEY TO EMOTIONAL LIBERATION: A TALE OF FOUR INDIVIDUALS

In the serene town of Meadowville, four individuals—Emma, Liam, Maya, and Ethan—found themselves entangled in the web of resentment and anger, each carrying their own burdensome emotions. However, destiny had something extraordinary in store for them, leading them on a transformative journey towards releasing their deep-rooted resentments and liberating themselves from the clutches of anger.

Emma, a warm-hearted schoolteacher, had been holding onto bitterness from a past betrayal. Liam, a hardworking businessman, was consumed by anger towards a colleague who had undermined him. Maya, a talented artist, carried the weight of resentment towards a family member's hurtful words. Ethan, a compassionate caregiver, struggled with long-held anger towards an absentee parent.

Their paths converged during a community workshop on emotional well-being, where they discovered the profound impact of releasing resentment and anger on their overall happiness and personal growth. Guided by a skilled facilitator, they embarked on a journey of self-reflection and forgiveness, eager to break free from the chains that bound them.

As they shared their stories and listened to one another's experiences, a sense of empathy and understanding enveloped the group. Through deep conversations and therapeutic exercises, they uncovered the underlying causes of their resentments and the ways in which anger had held them captive. With newfound clarity, they set their intentions to release these negative emotions and reclaim their emotional freedom.

Emma, with a compassionate heart, recognized that forgiveness was the key to releasing her resentment. She embarked on a profound inner dialogue, acknowledging her pain and the humanity of the person who had wronged her. Through forgiveness, she liberated herself from the burden of resentment, experiencing a newfound sense of peace and inner tranquility.

Liam, driven by a desire for personal growth, embraced the power of empathy and perspective-taking. He confronted the deep-seated anger towards his colleague by seeking to understand their motivations and challenges. As he cultivated empathy, he discovered the ability to forgive and let go, liberating himself from the toxic grip of anger and opening the door to healthier professional relationships.

Maya, the artist with a vivid imagination, found solace in creative expression. She channeled her resentment into her art, using vibrant colors and bold brushstrokes to externalize her emotions. With each stroke, she released the pent-up anger, allowing it to transform into a masterpiece of healing and catharsis.

Ethan, the empathetic caregiver, recognized that forgiveness was not solely directed towards others but also towards himself. He acknowledged that harboring anger towards his absentee parent only perpetuated his own suffering. Through self-compassion and a commitment to personal growth, he forgave himself for carrying the burden for so long, experiencing a newfound sense of liberation and self-acceptance.

As their individual journeys unfolded, Emma, Liam, Maya, and Ethan discovered the transformative power of releasing resentment and anger. They witnessed how the act of forgiveness not only set them free but also paved the way for deeper connections, enhanced well-being, and a renewed sense of joy in their lives.

Today, Emma, Liam, Maya, and Ethan stand as shining examples of the extraordinary strength that lies within each of us to release resentment and anger. Their collective journey reminds us that by acknowledging our emotions, embracing empathy and forgiveness, and finding healthy outlets for expression, we can break free from the chains of negativity and cultivate a life filled with love, understanding, and inner peace.

May their stories inspire us to embark on our own path of releasing resentment and anger, knowing that in doing so, we open ourselves up to a world of limitless possibilities and emotional liberation.

5.6 CONCLUSION

Releasing resentment and anger is an essential step in the forgiveness and letting go process. By understanding the destructive nature of resentment, learning techniques for managing these intense emotions, finding healthy outlets for their expression, and embracing the transformative power of forgiveness, we embark on a journey of emotional liberation and healing. Let us commit to releasing the toxic emotions that bind us, freeing ourselves to experience greater peace, joy, and fulfilling relationships.

5.7 REFLECTIVE EXERCISE

Take a moment to reflect on a specific situation or relationship where you have been holding onto resentment and anger. Allow yourself to fully acknowledge these emotions and their impact on your well-being.

In your journal or on a separate piece of paper, write down all the reasons why you have been holding onto resentment and anger in this particular situation. Be honest with yourself and explore the underlying causes and triggers that have contributed to these emotions.

Now, imagine the weight of resentment and anger being lifted from your shoulders. Visualize yourself releasing these negative emotions and replacing them with feelings of peace and freedom. How does it feel to let go of the burden of resentment and anger?

Next, consider healthy outlets for expressing and managing your emotions. Think of activities that can help you release pent-up anger or frustration, such as physical exercise, journaling, or talking to a trusted friend or therapist. Write down three or more strategies that resonate with you and commit to incorporating them into your routine.

Reflect on the cycle of hurt and how holding onto resentment and anger perpetuates it. Consider the potential for breaking this cycle through forgiveness. Ask yourself: What would it mean for me to forgive in this situation? How could forgiveness contribute to my emotional liberation and well-being?

Finally, envision a future where you have fully released resentment and anger in this situation. How does it impact your overall happiness and sense of inner peace? Write a short affirmation or mantra that encapsulates your commitment to releasing resentment and anger and embracing forgiveness.

Remember, releasing resentment and anger is a process that takes time and self-compassion. Be patient with yourself as you navigate through these emotions and continue to cultivate forgiveness. Use these reflective exercises as tools to support your journey of letting go and finding emotional liberation.

Note: If at any point you feel overwhelmed or stuck in this process, it is important to seek support from a mental health professional or counselor who can provide guidance and assistance tailored to your specific needs.

CHAPTER SIX

CULTIVATING EMPATHY AND UNDERSTANDING

IN THIS CHAPTER, we will explore the significance of cultivating empathy and understanding as integral components of the forgiveness and letting go process within familial and intimate relationships. By recognizing empathy as a key element, practicing active listening and open communication, seeking to understand the offender's perspective, and finding common ground to build bridges, we foster connection, empathy, and ultimately, the potential for forgiveness.

6.1 RECOGNIZING EMPATHY AS A KEY ELEMENT

Empathy is a key element when it comes to the journey of forgiveness and letting go within familial and intimate relationships. It plays a significant role in fostering healing and reconciliation. But what exactly is empathy?

Empathy goes beyond sympathy or feeling sorry for someone. It involves putting ourselves in the shoes of others, trying to understand their emotions, thoughts, and experiences without judgment. It requires us to listen attentively and validate their feelings. By doing so, we create a safe and supportive space for open communication and mutual understanding.

Recognizing empathy as a key element means acknowledging its importance in building deeper connections with others. It allows us to connect on a more profound level, to truly understand and appreciate the emotions and experiences of those we care about. Empathy helps us to bridge the gap between our own perspective and theirs, fostering compassion and empathy.

When we recognize empathy as a key element, we become more attuned to the emotions of others. We actively seek to understand their point of view, to see the world through their eyes. This requires setting aside our own biases and preconceptions, allowing us to approach situations with an open mind and heart.

Empathy is not always easy, especially when we have been hurt or wronged. It requires us to rise above our own pain and extend compassion to those who have hurt us. However, when we choose to embrace empathy, we create the potential for healing and growth within our relationships.

In summary, recognizing empathy as a key element in the forgiveness and letting go process is crucial for building understanding and connection within familial and intimate relationships. It allows us to step into the shoes of others, to truly understand and appreciate their emotions and experiences. By practicing empathy, we create a space for healing, compassion, and ultimately, the potential for forgiveness.

6.2 PRACTICING ACTIVE LISTENING AND OPEN COMMUNICATION

Practicing active listening and open communication is essential when cultivating empathy and understanding within familial and intimate relationships. It lays the foundation for meaningful and constructive dialogue, fostering mutual respect and deeper connections. But what does it mean to engage in active listening and open communication?

Active listening involves giving our full attention to the person speaking, without distractions or interruptions. It requires us to be present in the moment and genuinely interested in what the other person has to say. By actively listening, we demonstrate that we value their thoughts and feelings, creating an atmosphere of trust and openness.

Open communication, on the other hand, involves expressing ourselves honestly and authentically, while also being receptive to the perspectives of others. It means speaking our truth with kindness and respect, and actively inviting others to share their thoughts and emotions without fear of judgment. Open communication fosters an environment where everyone feels heard and understood.

When we practice active listening, we refrain from jumping to conclusions or interrupting with our own opinions. Instead, we give the speaker our undivided attention, maintaining eye contact and nodding to show that we are engaged. We also reflect back what we've heard to ensure we understand correctly and to validate the speaker's experience.

In open communication, we strive to create a safe space where all parties feel comfortable expressing themselves. We encourage open and honest dialogue by actively inviting others to share their thoughts and emotions. We approach conversations with curiosity and a genuine desire to understand, rather than simply waiting for our turn to speak.

By practicing active listening and open communication, we create an environment conducive to empathy and understanding. We foster trust and mutual respect, allowing each person to feel heard and validated. Through these practices, we bridge the gap between different perspectives and cultivate empathy, paving the way for healing and growth within our relationships.

In conclusion, practicing active listening and open communication is essential in cultivating empathy and understanding within familial and intimate relationships. These practices create a safe and supportive space for meaningful dialogue, where each person feels valued and heard. By engaging in active listening and open communication, we foster empathy, strengthen our connections, and open the door to forgiveness and healing.

6.3 SEEKING TO UNDERSTAND THE OFFENDER'S PERSPECTIVE

Seeking to understand the offender's perspective is a vital step in the process of cultivating empathy and understanding within familial and intimate relationships. It requires us to set aside our own preconceived notions and judgments, and approach the situation with an open mind and a genuine curiosity.

When we make an effort to understand the offender's perspective, we acknowledge their humanity and recognize that they, too, have their own experiences, emotions, and motivations. It does not mean condoning or excusing their actions, but rather striving to gain insight into their mindset and the factors that may have contributed to their behavior.

To seek understanding, we can start by engaging in compassionate and non-confrontational conversations with the offender. We listen attentively to their side of the story, allowing them to express themselves without interruption or judgment. By actively listening and asking open-ended questions, we create a safe space for them to share their thoughts and emotions.

It is important to approach these conversations with empathy and genuine curiosity. We strive to put ourselves in their shoes, imagining what it might have been like for them to experience the situation from their perspective. This exercise in empathy allows us to gain a deeper understanding of their motivations, fears, insecurities, or past experiences that may have influenced their actions.

In seeking to understand the offender's perspective, we aim to break down barriers and foster empathy. It helps us move beyond our own pain and resentment, and opens the possibility for healing and reconciliation. When we take the time to understand the offender, we create an opportunity for empathy to flourish, laying the groundwork for forgiveness and letting go.

However, it is important to note that seeking understanding does not mean we have to accept or agree with their perspective. We can still maintain our own boundaries and stand firm in our values. Seeking understanding is about expanding our perspective and developing empathy, not about compromising our own well-being or values.

In conclusion, seeking to understand the offender's perspective is a crucial aspect of cultivating empathy and understanding within familial and intimate relationships. It involves approaching conversations with compassion and openness, actively listening to their side of the story, and striving to see the situation through their eyes. By seeking understanding, we create space for empathy to grow, and pave the way for healing, forgiveness, and the possibility of rebuilding trust and connection.

6.4 FINDING COMMON GROUND TO BUILD BRIDGES

Finding common ground is a powerful tool in the process of cultivating empathy and understanding within familial and intimate relationships. It allows us to bridge the gap between ourselves and the offender, fostering connection and opening the door to forgiveness and letting go.

When we actively search for common ground, we look beyond our differences and focus on shared experiences, values, or goals. It helps us realize that, despite the conflicts and hurts that may have occurred, there are still areas where our interests align. By identifying these commonalities, we create a foundation for building understanding and empathy.

One way to find common ground is through open and honest communication. By engaging in meaningful conversations, we can uncover shared values or interests. This can be done by exploring topics that are important to both parties, such as family, personal growth, or the well-being of loved ones. When we discover common values or aspirations, it becomes easier to empathize with the offender and find areas of agreement.

Another approach is to focus on shared experiences or memories. Reflecting on positive moments or shared challenges can help create a sense of connection and remind us of the bond that exists between us. By revisiting these shared experiences, we tap into the reservoir of goodwill and compassion that can guide us towards forgiveness and understanding.

It is important to approach the search for common ground with an open mind and genuine intentions. We must be willing to listen and consider the perspectives and desires of the other person. By actively seeking commonalities, we show our commitment to finding resolution and rebuilding the relationship.

Finding common ground also requires flexibility and compromise. It may involve finding middle ground or making concessions to reach a mutually beneficial outcome. This does not mean compromising our values or boundaries, but rather finding areas where we can meet halfway and work towards a shared understanding.

By finding common ground, we build bridges of connection and understanding. It allows us to see the humanity in the offender and move beyond our differences. When we focus on shared experiences, values, or goals, we create a solid foundation for empathy, forgiveness, and the potential for reconciliation.

In conclusion, finding common ground is a powerful strategy for cultivating empathy and understanding in familial and intimate relationships. It involves actively seeking shared values, interests, or experiences that can bring us closer together. By recognizing our commonalities, we bridge the divide between ourselves and the offender, paving the way for healing, forgiveness, and the restoration of trust and connection.

6.5 CASE STUDY: THE EMPATHY CHRONICLES—A TALE OF THREE HEARTS

In the enchanting village of Ardmore, three individuals—Fiona, Liam, and Maeve—found themselves entangled in a web of misunderstandings and longing for deeper connections and a more empathetic world. Little did they know that their paths would converge, leading them on a transformative journey of cultivating empathy and understanding.

Fiona, a compassionate nurse, had witnessed the power of empathy in her professional life but struggled to extend it to her personal relationships. Liam, a spirited artist, often grappled with expressing his emotions, yearning for others to understand his creative perspective. Maeve, a wise grandmother, carried the weight of past hurts and longed for reconciliation and understanding within her family.

Destiny brought them together at an intimate gathering celebrating the art of empathy. Through heartfelt conversations, shared experiences, and thought-provoking exercises, they embarked on a profound journey of self-reflection and growth, seeking to cultivate empathy and understanding within themselves and their relationships.

Fiona, with her nurturing spirit, embarked on a quest to truly understand the experiences and emotions of others. Through deep listening, genuine empathy, and acts of kindness, she created a safe space for vulnerability and connection. As Fiona embraced the power of empathy, her relationships blossomed, fostering a sense of belonging and understanding in her community.

Liam, the expressive artist, discovered a unique medium to cultivate empathy and understanding—his art. Through his captivating paintings and sculptures, he unveiled the depths of human emotions, inviting others to connect with their own experiences. As his artwork sparked conversations and opened hearts, Liam witnessed the transformative power of creativity in fostering empathy and bridging divides.

Maeve, the wise grandmother, embarked on a journey of healing and forgiveness, seeking to understand the perspectives of her loved ones. Through open-hearted conversations and gentle guidance, she nurtured an atmosphere of empathy within her family. As Maeve let go of past resentments and embraced forgiveness, she witnessed the restoration of bonds and the emergence of empathy among generations.

The journeys of Fiona, Liam, and Maeve beautifully illustrate the transformative power of cultivating empathy and understanding. They serve as inspirations, reminding us that by embracing empathy, actively listening, and seeking to understand one another, we can create profound connections and foster a more compassionate and harmonious world.

Their stories invite us to embark on our own paths of empathy and understanding, knowing that small acts of compassion, genuine curiosity, and open hearts have the power to mend relationships, bridge divides, and ignite a positive change in our communities.

6.6 CONCLUSION

In conclusion, cultivating empathy and understanding is paramount in the process of forgiveness and letting go within familial and intimate relationships. Recognizing empathy as a key element, practicing active listening and open communication, seeking to understand the offender's perspective, and finding common ground to build bridges all contribute to fostering connection, empathy, and the potential for forgiveness. By nurturing these qualities, we create a space for healing, understanding, and the possibility of building stronger, more compassionate relationships.

6.7 REFLECTIVE EXERCISE

Take a moment to reflect on a specific situation or relationship where empathy and understanding have been lacking. Consider the challenges you have faced in truly understanding the perspective of the other person involved.

In your journal or on a separate piece of paper, write down your initial thoughts and feelings about the situation. Reflect on any biases or preconceived notions you may hold that hinder your ability to cultivate empathy and understanding.

Now, put yourself in the other person's shoes. Imagine their experiences, emotions, and motivations that may have influenced their actions or behavior. How does it feel to see the situation from their perspective?

Next, think about the barriers to open communication and active listening that may have hindered your ability to cultivate empathy and understanding. Identify any assumptions, judgments, or emotional blocks that have kept you from truly connecting with the other person.

Consider ways to enhance empathy and understanding in this situation. Write down three or more strategies that you can practice to improve your ability to listen attentively, validate the other person's feelings, and find common ground for mutual understanding.

Reflect on the potential benefits of cultivating empathy and understanding in this specific relationship. How could it contribute to building bridges, fostering connection, and creating a more harmonious dynamic?

Finally, envision a future where empathy and understanding are at the forefront of your interactions in this relationship. How does it impact the quality of your connection and the potential for forgiveness? Write a short affirmation or mantra that reinforces your commitment to cultivating empathy and understanding.

Remember, cultivating empathy and understanding is an ongoing practice that requires patience, openness, and genuine curiosity. Use these reflective exercises as tools to support your journey of fostering connection and cultivating forgiveness through empathy and understanding.

Note: If you find it challenging to cultivate empathy or navigate complex emotions within this relationship, consider seeking support from a mental health professional or counselor who can provide guidance and help you develop the necessary skills for empathy and understanding.

CHAPTER SEVEN

THE POWER OF SELF-FORGIVENESS

In this chapter, we will explore the transformative power of self-forgiveness within the forgiveness and letting go process within familial and intimate relationships. By recognizing the need for self-forgiveness, letting go of guilt and shame, embracing imperfection and growth, and practicing self-compassion and self-love, we embark on a journey of healing, personal growth, and inner peace.

7.1 RECOGNIZING THE NEED FOR SELF-FORGIVENESS

Self-forgiveness is a crucial aspect of the forgiveness and letting go process within familial and intimate relationships. Often, we are quick to forgive others while being harsh and unforgiving towards ourselves. However, recognizing the need for self-forgiveness is essential for our emotional well-being and the health of our relationships.

Many of us carry the weight of past mistakes, regrets, and perceived shortcomings. We may hold onto guilt, shame, and self-blame, which can create a barrier to self-acceptance and hinder our personal growth. It is important to understand that we are human, and as humans, we are imperfect. We make mistakes, and we learn from them.

Recognizing the need for self-forgiveness involves acknowledging our own humanity and embracing our imperfections. It requires understanding that holding onto guilt and self-blame serves no purpose other than keeping us stuck in a cycle of negativity. We deserve to free ourselves from the burden of self-condemnation and allow ourselves to move forward with compassion and self-love.

Self-forgiveness does not mean denying responsibility for our actions or dismissing the consequences of our behavior. It is about accepting what has happened, taking accountability, and learning from our mistakes. It is a process of acknowledging the pain we may have caused ourselves or others and making a conscious decision to release ourselves from the grip of guilt and self-judgment.

To begin the journey of self-forgiveness, we must be willing to let go of the past and embrace the present moment. It is essential to recognize that we have the power to change and grow, and that our past does not define us. We can learn from our mistakes and use them as opportunities for personal growth and transformation.

Practicing self-compassion and self-love is an integral part of self-forgiveness. It involves treating ourselves with kindness, understanding, and patience. We need to cultivate an inner dialogue that is supportive and nurturing, rather than critical and punishing. Self-compassion allows us to offer ourselves the same level of forgiveness and understanding that we would extend to others.

It is important to remember that self-forgiveness is a journey, not an instant destination. It may take time and effort to release ourselves fully from the grip of self-blame and guilt. It requires consistent practice and self-reflection. However, through self-forgiveness, we open the doors to healing, personal growth, and inner peace.

In conclusion, recognizing the need for self-forgiveness is an essential step in the forgiveness and letting go process within familial and intimate relationships. By acknowledging our own humanity, embracing imperfection, practicing self-compassion, and letting go of guilt and shame, we embark on a transformative journey of healing, personal growth, and inner peace. Self-forgiveness is a gift we give ourselves, allowing us to move forward with love and acceptance for ourselves and others.

7.2 LETTING GO OF GUILT AND SHAME

Guilt and shame are powerful emotions that can weigh heavily on our hearts and minds. They can create a sense of unworthiness, self-condemnation, and hinder our ability to forgive ourselves. In the forgiveness and letting go process within familial and intimate relationships, it is crucial to address and release guilt and shame for our own well-being and growth.

Guilt is the feeling we experience when we believe we have done something wrong or violated our own moral code. It serves as a reminder that our actions have conse-quences and can motivate us to make amends and change our behavior. However, when guilt becomes excessive or disproportionate to the situation, it can become debilitating and prevent us from moving forward.

Shame, on the other hand, is a deep-seated belief that we are fundamentally flawed or unworthy as individuals. It goes beyond feeling bad about our actions and encom-passes a sense of inherent inadequacy. Shame can be rooted in past experiences, societal expectations, or self-imposed standards of perfection.

To let go of guilt and shame, we must first acknowledge and accept these emotions. It is important to recognize that experiencing guilt or shame does not define us as individuals. We are capable of growth, learning, and change. Mistakes and shortcomings are a natural part of being human, and they do not diminish our worth or value as individuals.

One effective way to release guilt and shame is through self-reflection and understanding. It involves examining the underlying reasons for our actions, understanding the context in which they occurred, and taking responsi-bility for our behavior. It is essential to separate the action from our sense of self-worth. We can acknowledge that we made a mistake without believing that we are inherently bad or unworthy.

Practicing self-compassion is a powerful tool in letting go of guilt and shame. It means treating ourselves with kindness, understanding, and forgiveness. We can offer ourselves the same level of compassion and understanding that we would extend to a loved one who has made a mistake. Self-compassion allows us to learn from our actions, make amends if necessary, and grow from the experience.

Forgiveness, both of ourselves and others, is a key component in releasing guilt and shame. It involves recognizing that holding onto these negative emotions only serves to keep us stuck in the past. Forgiveness does not mean condoning the actions or dismissing the consequences; rather, it is a conscious choice to release ourselves from the burden of guilt and shame. It is a process of letting go and embracing the possibility of growth, healing, and self-acceptance.

Letting go of guilt and shame requires patience and self-care. It may involve seeking support from trusted friends, family, or professionals who can offer guidance and understanding. Engaging in self-care activities such as journaling, practicing mindfulness, and engaging in hobbies that bring us joy can also help in the healing process.

In conclusion, letting go of guilt and shame is an important step in the journey of self-forgiveness and personal growth. By acknowledging these emotions, practicing self-reflection, cultivating self-compassion, and embracing the power of forgiveness, we free ourselves from the weight of guilt and shame. We open the doors to self-acceptance, healing, and the ability to move forward with renewed hope and a sense of empowerment.

7.3 EMBRACING IMPERFECTION AND GROWTH

In our journey towards self-forgiveness and personal growth, it is essential to embrace the concepts of imperfection and growth. Oftentimes, we hold ourselves to unrealistic standards and expect perfection in every aspect of our lives. However, this pursuit of perfection can be a source of self-criticism, disappointment, and hinder our ability to forgive ourselves.

Embracing imperfection means recognizing that we are human beings with flaws, limitations, and a unique set of strengths and weaknesses. It is about letting go of the unrealistic expectations we place on ourselves and acknowledging that making mistakes is a natural part of the learning and growth process. By accepting our imperfections, we create space for self-compassion, understanding, and forgiveness.

Growth, on the other hand, is a lifelong journey of continuous development, learning, and personal evolution. It is an acknowledgment that we have the capacity to change, improve, and become better versions of ourselves. Growth involves stepping out of our comfort zones, facing challenges, and embracing new opportunities for self-discovery and self-improvement.

To embrace imperfection and growth, it is important to cultivate a mindset of self-acceptance and self-compassion. Instead of berating ourselves for our mistakes or shortcomings, we can choose to approach them with curiosity and a willingness to learn. We can view them as valuable lessons that contribute to our personal growth and development.

One helpful strategy is to reframe our perception of failure. Rather than seeing failure as a reflection of our worth or competence, we can view it as an opportunity for growth and self-improvement. By reframing failure as a stepping stone towards success, we can foster resilience, perseverance, and a positive mindset.

It is also crucial to set realistic expectations for ourselves. Instead of striving for perfection in every aspect of our lives, we can focus on progress and personal growth. This involves celebrating our achievements, no matter how small, and acknowledging the effort and dedication we put into our self-improvement journey.

Embracing imperfection and growth also requires embracing vulnerability. It means allowing ourselves to be authentic, to acknowledge our limitations, and to seek help when needed. Opening ourselves up to vulnerability allows us to connect with others on a deeper level and foster meaningful relationships built on trust, empathy, and understanding.

Lastly, it is important to remember that self-forgiveness and personal growth are not linear processes. There will be ups and downs, setbacks and breakthroughs. It is okay to stumble along the way. What matters is our commitment to embracing imperfection, nurturing a growth mindset, and continuing to move forward on our journey of self-discovery and self-forgiveness.

In conclusion, embracing imperfection and growth is a powerful step in the process of self-forgiveness and personal growth. By letting go of unrealistic expectations, cultivating self-compassion, reframing failure, setting realistic goals, embracing vulnerability, and embracing the journey of continuous growth, we free ourselves from the shackles of self-criticism and open ourselves up to a life of authenticity, fulfillment, and self-acceptance.

7.4 PRACTICING SELF-COMPASSION AND SELF-LOVE

In the journey of self-forgiveness and personal growth, one of the most important practices we can embrace is that of self-compassion and self-love. Often, we are quick to extend kindness, understanding, and forgiveness to others, yet struggle to offer the same compassion to ourselves. However, cultivating self-compassion and self-love is crucial for our well-being, healing, and the process of forgiveness.

Self-compassion is about treating ourselves with the same kindness, care, and understanding that we would offer to a dear friend who is going through a difficult time. It involves acknowledging our own pain, struggles, and imperfections with empathy and gentleness. Rather than criticizing or judging ourselves harshly, self-compassion allows us to embrace our humanity and respond with kindness and support.

To practice self-compassion, we can start by cultivating self-awareness. This involves paying attention to our thoughts, emotions, and the way we talk to ourselves. Notice when self-critical or judgmental thoughts arise and gently redirect them towards self-compassionate and understanding perspectives. Treat yourself with the same warmth and empathy you would extend to a loved one in need.

Another essential aspect of self-compassion is self-care. Taking care of our physical, emotional, and mental well-being is a powerful way to demonstrate self-love. Engage in activities that nourish your body, mind, and soul. This can include engaging in hobbies, spending time in nature, practicing mindfulness or meditation, seeking support from loved ones, or seeking professional help when needed.

It's important to remember that self-compassion doesn't mean disregarding personal growth or accountability. It is not about excusing harmful behaviors or avoiding necessary changes. Instead, self-compassion helps us approach our shortcomings and mistakes with understanding and a commitment to growth. It allows us to learn from our experiences, make amends when necessary, and cultivate a sense of forgiveness and acceptance towards ourselves.

Practicing self-love is closely intertwined with self-compassion. It involves developing a deep appreciation and acceptance of who we are, embracing our strengths, and embracing our flaws. Self-love is recognizing our inherent worthiness and treating ourselves with kindness, respect, and care.

One powerful way to practice self-love is through positive self-talk and affirmations. Replace self-critical thoughts with affirmations that uplift and empower you. Remind yourself of your strengths, accomplishments, and unique qualities. Treat yourself as your own best friend and advocate, offering words of encouragement and support.

Setting boundaries is another important aspect of self-love. Learn to prioritize your needs and well-being, and communicate them assertively to others. This allows you to create a safe and nurturing environment for yourself, free from resentment or the burden of constantly people-pleasing.

Lastly, practicing self-compassion and self-love involves cultivating a mindset of self-acceptance. Embrace all aspects of yourself, including your past mistakes, vulnerabilities, and perceived flaws. Recognize that you are a work in progress, and that growth and learning are part of the human experience. Embrace self-forgiveness as a way to let go of self-blame and open yourself up to growth, healing, and personal transformation.

In conclusion, practicing self-compassion and self-love is essential for self-forgiveness and personal growth. By treating ourselves with kindness, understanding, and acceptance, we create an inner environment of love and healing. Through self-awareness, self-care, positive self-talk, setting boundaries, and cultivating self-acceptance, we nourish our well-being and create a foundation for forgiveness, growth, and a life filled with self-compassion and love.

7.5 CASE STUDY: THE JOURNEY TO SELF-FORGIVENESS: A TALE OF FOUR SOULS

In the picturesque town of Larksville, four individuals—Elena, Marcus, Nora, and Finn—found themselves entangled in the complex web of self-judgment, guilt, and the longing for self-forgiveness. Little did they know that their paths would intertwine, leading them on a transformative journey of self-discovery, healing, and the profound power of self-forgiveness.

Elena, a talented pianist, had carried the weight of a past mistake that haunted her every performance. Marcus, a dedicated teacher, found himself trapped in a cycle of self-blame for a decision he made in his classroom. Nora, a compassionate caregiver, struggled with guilt for not being able to meet the needs of her loved ones. Finn, a passionate writer, battled with self-doubt and the lingering pain of rejection.

Destiny brought them together at a therapeutic retreat, where they embarked on a profound journey of self-exploration and healing. Guided by the compassionate facilitator, Dr. Harper, they delved deep into their past experiences, exploring the roots of their self-judgment and guilt.

Through introspection, vulnerability, and the power of self-reflection, Elena discovered the strength to release her self-imposed burden, allowing her music to flow freely once again. Marcus, with the support of the group, found solace in embracing his imperfections and learned to forgive himself for his perceived failure. Nora, through compassionate self-care, learned to forgive herself for not being able to be everything to everyone, understanding that she too deserved love and understanding. Finn, through the cathartic process of writing, found the courage to let go of his past rejections and embrace his unique voice.

As they journeyed through their individual paths of self-forgiveness, Elena, Marcus, Nora, and Finn realized that self-forgiveness was not about erasing their past mistakes but about accepting their humanity, embracing growth, and nurturing self-compassion. They witnessed the transformative power of self-forgiveness, as it opened doors to personal freedom, self-acceptance, and renewed purpose in their lives.

Their stories inspire us to embark on our own journeys of self-forgiveness, recognizing that we all carry the weight of our past actions and decisions. By embracing self-compassion, acknowledging our mistakes, and committing to personal growth, we can break free from the shackles of guilt and self-judgment, paving the way for inner healing, emotional well-being, and a renewed sense of self.

May the stories of Elena, Marcus, Nora, and Finn remind us of the profound power of self-forgiveness, offering hope and inspiration on our own paths of self-discovery, acceptance, and the beautiful journey towards embracing our imperfect, yet deeply deserving, selves.

7.6 CONCLUSION

The power of self-forgiveness is a transformative force that holds the key to our inner healing and personal growth. Through the journey of self-forgiveness, we learn to release the burdens of guilt, shame, and self-judgment that weigh us down. By embracing self-compassion, accepting our imperfections, and acknowledging our humanity, we pave the way for a profound shift in our relationship with ourselves. Self-forgiveness grants us the freedom to let go of the past, nurture self-love, and create a future filled with inner peace, resilience, and the limitless potential to thrive. May we all find the strength and courage to embark on the empowering journey of self-forgiveness, embracing the power to heal, grow, and truly forgive ourselves.

7.7 REFLECTIVE EXERCISE

Take a moment to reflect on a specific situation or mistake from your past where you have been holding onto guilt or shame. Allow yourself to fully acknowledge the weight of these emotions and the impact they have had on your well-being.

In your journal or on a separate piece of paper, write a letter to yourself, expressing forgiveness for the mistake or action that has been causing you guilt or shame. Be compassionate and understanding as you write, acknowledging your humanity and the lessons you have learned from the experience.

Next, reflect on the reasons why you have been holding onto guilt or shame. What beliefs or expectations have contributed to your self-judgment? Write them down and consider whether they are serving your growth and well-being.

Now, challenge these beliefs and expectations by writing down alternative, more compassionate perspectives. Focus on the lessons learned, the growth you have experienced, and the opportunities for self-improvement that have emerged from the situation.

Practice self-compassion by engaging in self-care activities that nurture your physical, mental, and emotional well-being. This could include journaling, engaging in hobbies you enjoy, spending time in nature, practicing mindfulness or meditation, or seeking support from loved ones or a therapist.

Consider what self-forgiveness means to you and how it can contribute to your personal growth and inner peace. Write down affirmations or mantras that promote self-forgiveness and self-acceptance. Repeat them regularly to reinforce a positive and compassionate mindset.

Lastly, reflect on the potential impact of self-forgiveness on your relationships with others. How does forgiving yourself and embracing self-love influence your ability to forgive others and cultivate healthier connections?

Remember, self-forgiveness is a journey that requires patience, self-reflection, and self-compassion. Use these reflective exercises as tools to support your ongoing process of self-forgiveness and to embrace personal growth, inner peace, and self-love.

CHAPTER EIGHT

THE ART OF LETTING GO

IN THIS CHAPTER, we will explore the transformative process of letting go as an essential aspect of the forgiveness and healing journey within familial and intimate relationships. By understanding the significance of letting go, detaching emotionally from the past, releasing attachments to the offense and offender, forgiving yourself for holding on, and creating rituals and symbolic acts to symbolize letting go, we open ourselves to new possibilities, growth, and inner peace.

8.1 DETACHING EMOTIONALLY FROM THE PAST

Detaching emotionally from the past is an essential aspect of the art of letting go. It is the process of releasing our emotional attachments to past events, experiences, and relationships. By detaching ourselves, we free ourselves from the grip of negative emotions, allowing space for healing, growth, and the possibility of forgiveness.

When we hold onto the past, we carry the weight of emotional baggage that hinders our present and future. We may find ourselves trapped in a cycle of resentment, anger, and pain, unable to move forward. Detaching emotionally means consciously choosing to break free from this cycle and reclaim our emotional well-being.

One way to detach emotionally is by acknowledging and accepting the past as an integral part of our journey. It is essential to recognize that while the past has shaped us, it does not define our present or dictate our future. By embracing this perspective, we create room for new experiences and possibilities.

Another crucial step in detaching emotionally is practicing self-awareness. This involves becoming mindful of our emotions and thoughts related to the past. By observing these emotions without judgment, we can begin to understand their impact on our well-being. Through self-awareness, we gain the power to choose how we respond to these emotions, rather than being controlled by them.

Letting go of the need for closure or resolution is also a significant part of detaching emotionally. Sometimes, we hold onto the past because we seek answers or justice. However, clinging to these desires can keep us stuck and prevent us from moving forward. Accepting that closure may not always be attainable allows us to shift our focus towards our own healing and growth.

Forgiveness plays a crucial role in detaching emotionally from the past. It is a choice to release the resentment and anger we may hold towards those who have hurt us. Forgiveness does not mean condoning the actions or forgetting what happened, but rather, it is a decision to let go of the emotional burden that keeps us tied to the past. By forgiving, we free ourselves from the negative energy and open ourselves up to healing.

Practicing self-care and nurturing ourselves is also vital in the process of detaching emotionally. Engaging in activities that bring us joy, seeking support from loved ones or professionals, and prioritizing our mental and emotional well-being can help us in releasing the emotional attachments. Taking care of ourselves allows us to build resilience and strength as we navigate the journey of letting go.

In conclusion, detaching emotionally from the past is a powerful step in the art of letting go. By acknowledging the past's impact without letting it define us, practicing self-awareness, letting go of the need for closure, embracing forgiveness, and prioritizing self-care, we liberate ourselves from the chains of negative emotions. Detaching emotionally opens up space for healing, growth, and the possibility of forging healthier relationships and finding inner peace.

8.2 RELEASING ATTACHMENTS TO THE OFFENSE AND OFFENDER

Releasing attachments to the offense and offender is a crucial step in the art of letting go. When we hold onto these attachments, we keep ourselves bound to the past, hindering our ability to move forward, heal, and find peace. By consciously releasing these attachments, we create space for forgiveness, personal growth, and the restoration of emotional well-being.

Attachments to the offense and offender can take many forms. We may cling to feelings of anger, resentment, or even a desire for revenge. These attachments can consume our thoughts and emotions, keeping us trapped in a cycle of negativity and preventing us from experiencing true freedom.

To release attachments, we must first acknowledge the impact they have on our lives. Recognizing that holding onto these attachments only perpetuates our suffering is an important realization. It allows us to shift our focus towards our own well-being rather than being consumed by thoughts and emotions tied to the offense and offender.

One powerful strategy for releasing attachments is practicing forgiveness. Forgiveness is a choice to let go of the anger, resentment, and desire for retribution towards the offender. It does not mean condoning their actions or forgetting what happened, but rather, it is a decision to free ourselves from the emotional burden that keeps us tethered to the past. Forgiveness is an act of self-empowerment and liberation.

Another helpful approach is cultivating empathy and compassion. This involves trying to understand the offender's perspective and the factors that may have contributed to their actions. While it may be challenging, recognizing the common humanity in all individuals can help soften our attachments and foster a sense of compassion. Empathy allows us to see beyond the surface and acknowledge the complex layers of human experience.

It is also essential to focus on our own personal growth and healing. By investing our energy and attention into our own well-being, we shift our focus away from the offense and offender. Engaging in self-reflection, seeking therapy or counseling, and pursuing activities that bring us joy and fulfillment can contribute to our growth and help us let go of the attachments that no longer serve us.

Letting go of attachments can be a gradual process that requires patience and self-compassion. It is important to give ourselves permission to feel and acknowledge the emotions that arise during this journey. By honoring our emotions and allowing ourselves to grieve, heal, and process, we create a solid foundation for releasing attachments and embracing personal transformation.

In conclusion, releasing attachments to the offense and offender is an integral part of the art of letting go. By acknowledging the impact of these attachments, practicing forgiveness, cultivating empathy and compassion, and prioritizing personal growth and healing, we break free from the chains that bind us to the past. Releasing attachments opens up space for forgiveness, personal growth, and the restoration of emotional well-being. It empowers us to embrace the present and build a future free from the burdens of the past.

8.3 FORGIVING YOURSELF FOR HOLDING ON

Forgiving yourself for holding on is an essential step in the art of letting go. Often, we find ourselves trapped in the past, clinging to emotions, regrets, or blame that prevent us from moving forward and finding peace. By offering yourself forgiveness, you can release the burden of self-judgment and create space for healing and personal growth.

When we hold on to past hurts, we may berate ourselves for not letting go sooner or for allowing the pain to affect us deeply. We may carry guilt and self-blame for our perceived role in the situation or for not forgiving ourselves earlier. However, it is important to recognize that holding on is a natural response to pain, and forgiving yourself is a powerful act of self-compassion.

To begin the process of self-forgiveness, it is crucial to acknowledge your emotions and experiences without judgment. Allow yourself to feel the pain, anger, or sadness that may arise from holding on. Accept that these emotions are valid and part of your healing journey. Remember that you are human, and it is natural to have a range of emotions in response to challenging situations.

Next, practice self-reflection and self-compassion. Take time to understand why you held on and what needs or fears were at play. Recognize that you were doing the best you could with the resources and understanding you had at that time. Instead of blaming yourself, offer yourself kindness and understanding. Remind yourself that you deserve love, forgiveness, and healing just like anyone else.

As you cultivate self-compassion, challenge any self-limiting beliefs or negative self-talk. Replace self-criticism with affirmations of self-worth and resilience. Remind yourself that holding on was a part of your journey, and now you are ready to let go and embrace a new chapter of healing and growth.

Another helpful practice is reframing your perspective. Instead of seeing holding on as a failure, view it as an opportunity for learning and growth. Reflect on the lessons you have gained from this experience and how it has shaped you into a stronger, more resilient person. Recognize that forgiveness is a process, and it takes time and patience. Allow yourself the space to heal and forgive at your own pace.

Engaging in self-care activities can also support the process of self-forgiveness. Nurture your mind, body, and soul through activities that bring you joy, relaxation, and peace. This could include practicing mindfulness, engaging in hobbies, spending time in nature, or seeking support from loved ones or professionals.

Remember, self-forgiveness is a gift you give to yourself. It is an act of releasing self-judgment and embracing self-love. By forgiving yourself for holding on, you break free from the chains of the past and create space for healing, growth, and inner peace.

In conclusion, forgiving yourself for holding on is a crucial step in the art of letting go. It allows you to release self-judgment, embrace self-compassion, and create space for healing and personal growth. Remember that you are deserving of forgiveness and love. By practicing self-reflection, self-compassion, reframing your perspective, and engaging in self-care, you can embark on a transformative journey of self-forgiveness. Embrace the present moment, let go of the past, and cultivate a future filled with inner peace and emotional liberation.

8.4 CREATING RITUALS AND SYMBOLIC ACTS TO SYMBOLIZE LETTING GO

Creating rituals and symbolic acts can be powerful tools in the process of letting go. When we attach meaning to our actions, we give ourselves the opportunity to release emotional burdens, invite closure, and symbolize the act of moving forward. These rituals and symbolic acts serve as tangible reminders of our commitment to letting go and embracing new beginnings.

One effective way to create a ritual of letting go is through writing. Take a moment to reflect on what you are ready to release and let go of. Write down your thoughts, emotions, or any lingering attachments related to the situation. Be honest with yourself and express everything you need to let go of. Once you have poured your heart out onto the paper, you can choose to burn or shred it as a symbolic act of releasing those emotions. As the paper transforms into ashes or strips, visualize the weight of the past being lifted from your shoulders, allowing space for healing and growth.

Another meaningful ritual is the act of visualization. Find a quiet and comfortable space where you can sit undisturbed. Close your eyes and visualize the situation or emotions you want to let go of. Imagine them as physical objects or energy within you. As you breathe deeply, visualize yourself gently releasing these objects or energy, watching them float away or dissolve into the distance. Feel the lightness and freedom that comes with letting go, allowing yourself to embrace a renewed sense of peace and possibility.

Physical acts of releasing can also be powerful. Consider engaging in activities such as decluttering your living space, rearranging furniture, or donating items that no longer serve you. As you remove physical reminders of the past, you create space for new energy to flow into your life. Additionally, engaging in activities like painting, drawing, or sculpting can provide a creative outlet for expressing and releasing emotions associated with the situation. Let your creativity guide you as you externalize your inner process of letting go.

Nature can also offer a profound backdrop for symbolic acts of letting go. Find a serene outdoor location, such as a park, beach, or forest. Take a walk and find a natural object that represents what you want to release. It could be a leaf, a stone, or any other item that resonates with you. Hold the object in your hands, infusing it with the emotions and attachments you wish to let go of. Then, with intention, release the object into a body of water, let it float away on a breeze, or bury it in the earth. As you do so, visualize the act of releasing and feel a sense of liberation and renewal.

Remember, rituals and symbolic acts are personal and unique to each individual. Choose practices that resonate with you and align with your beliefs and values. The intention behind these acts is what matters most. Whether it's through writing, visualization, physical acts, or connecting with nature, the purpose is to create a tangible representation of your commitment to let go and move forward.

In conclusion, creating rituals and symbolic acts to symbolize letting go can be a powerful and transformative process. These acts provide us with a tangible way to release emotional burdens, invite closure, and embrace new beginnings. Through writing, visualization, physical acts, or connecting with nature, we externalize our inner process of letting go and create space for healing, growth, and renewal. Find the rituals that resonate with you, infuse them with intention, and embrace the transformative power of letting go.

8.5 CASE STUDY: THE JOURNEY OF LETTING GO

In the case study of Emma Thompson, Jason Rodriguez, and Sarah Johnson, we witness the transformative power of letting go explored in this chapter. These individuals faced unique challenges that required them to detach emotionally from their past, release attachments to their pain, and forgive themselves for holding on. Under the guidance of a supportive therapist, they embarked on their respective journeys of healing and growth.

Emma Thompson, a dedicated businesswoman, struggled with the failure of her business venture. Through therapy and introspection, she discovered that her self-worth was not defined by this setback. Emma embraced the lessons learned from her mistakes and found the courage to pursue new opportunities, igniting a sense of purpose and reinvention in her life.

Jason Rodriguez found himself trapped in a toxic relationship that hindered his personal growth. With the help of therapy, he realized the importance of letting go for his own well-being. Jason gradually understood his value and set boundaries, freeing himself from the toxicity and opening doors to healthier connections and self-discovery through his art.

Sarah Johnson carried deep wounds from a painful past and struggled to forgive herself for past mistakes. Through therapy and self-compassion practices, she confronted her feelings of guilt and shame, learning that everyone makes mistakes and deserves forgiveness, including herself. Sarah's journey of self-forgiveness brought about a renewed sense of joy, purpose, and healthier relationships with her loved ones.

The outcomes of their journeys were remarkable. Emma, Jason, and Sarah experienced personal transformations that aligned with the principles of letting go explored in Chapter 8. Their resilience and willingness to embrace change allowed them to move forward and create brighter futures for themselves.

The case study of Emma, Jason, and Sarah serves as a testament to the power of letting go. It illustrates the significance of detaching from the past, releasing attachments, and forgiving oneself for holding on. Their stories inspire others to embark on their own paths of letting go, finding healing, and creating a more fulfilling and peaceful life.

8.6 CONCLUSION

In conclusion, the art of letting go is a profound and transformative process that enables us to break free from the shackles of resentment, anger, and pain. It is through this process that we open ourselves to the possibilities of healing, growth, and inner peace within our familial and intimate relationships. By detaching emotionally from the past, releasing attachments, forgiving ourselves, and creating symbolic acts of letting go, we embark on a journey of self-discovery, personal liberation, and the rekindling of love and connection. As we embrace the power of letting go, we pave the way for a brighter future filled with understanding, compassion, and authentic joy. Letting go is an ongoing practice, and as we continue to cultivate the art of letting go, we cultivate a life of profound freedom, authenticity, and love.

8.7 REFLECTIVE EXERCISE

Take a few moments to reflect on a situation or past hurt that you have been holding onto tightly. Allow yourself to fully acknowledge the emotions and attachments associated with this situation.

In your journal or on a separate piece of paper, write a letter to the person or situation involved, expressing your feelings, frustrations, and the impact it has had on your life. Be honest and authentic in your writing, allowing yourself to release any pent-up emotions.

Next, reflect on the reasons why you have been holding onto this hurt or attachment. What beliefs, fears, or insecurities have contributed to your resistance to letting go? Write them down and consider whether they are serving your well-being and growth.

Now, challenge these beliefs and fears by writing down alternative, empowering perspectives. Focus on the lessons learned, the personal growth you have experienced, and the potential for positive change that can come from releasing this attachment.

Consider creating a symbolic act or ritual to represent the act of letting go. This could involve writing down the hurtful situation on a piece of paper and then burning or tearing it apart, symbolizing the release of its hold on you. Alternatively, you could engage in a physical activity like hiking or releasing a balloon, visualizing the act of releasing and letting go.

Reflect on the potential benefits of letting go in your life. How would releasing this attachment free up mental and emotional space for new experiences and positive growth? Write down your insights and intentions for moving forward.

Practice self-care and self-compassion as you navigate the process of letting go. Engage in activities that bring you joy, seek support from loved ones or a therapist, and prioritize your emotional well-being.

Remember, letting go is a gradual process that requires patience and self-compassion. Use these reflective exercises as tools to support your journey of letting go, and embrace the transformative power of releasing attachments, finding inner peace, and opening yourself up to new possibilities.

CHAPTER NINE

MOVING FORWARD AND REBUILDING TRUST

IN THIS CHAPTER, we will explore the essential steps to move forward and rebuild trust within familial and intimate relationships after experiencing hurt and forgiveness. By focusing on rebuilding trust, establishing boundaries and healthy communication, learning from the experience and growing stronger, and nurturing a positive future, we lay the foundation for a renewed and healthier connection.

9.1 THE IMPORTANCE OF REBUILDING TRUST

Rebuilding trust in relationships is crucial when it has been broken. Trust forms the foundation of a strong and meaningful connection with others. When trust is lost, it can lead to hurt and a sense of disconnection. However, rebuilding trust is important for letting go of the past and moving forward in familial and intimate relationships.

Rebuilding trust helps to create a safe and secure environment. When trust is shattered, people may feel vulnerable and find it difficult to let go of past hurts. By actively working on rebuilding trust, partners can provide reassurance and consistency, helping both individuals feel safe enough to let go of the pain and build a stronger connection.

Restoring trust also deepens intimacy and connection. Rebuilding trust allows partners to be more open and honest with each other. It encourages authentic communication and enables individuals to express their vulnerabilities and fears. By rebuilding trust, couples can cultivate a deeper sense of closeness and understanding, reigniting the bond that may have been strained.

Rebuilding trust promotes emotional healing and personal growth. When trust is broken, it causes emotional wounds that need to be addressed. Rebuilding trust provides an opportunity for individuals to have honest conversations, listen actively, and show empathy. Through this process, people can let go of past hurts and grow emotionally. It allows for learning from experiences, developing resilience, and becoming more capable of forgiveness and personal growth.

Furthermore, rebuilding trust creates a solid foundation for the future. It shows a commitment to growth and resilience within the relationship. By actively participating in rebuilding trust, individuals demonstrate their dedication to the long-term success of the relationship. It sets the stage for a future built on trust, respect, and shared goals.

In conclusion, rebuilding trust is vital for letting go of the past and moving forward in familial and intimate relationships. It helps create a safe and secure environment, deepens intimacy, promotes emotional healing, and establishes a foundation for a resilient and thriving relationship. Rebuilding trust requires effort, patience, and open communication, but the rewards are immeasurable. By recognizing the importance of rebuilding trust, individuals can embark on a transformative journey of healing, personal growth, and the restoration of a strong and meaningful connection.

9.2 ESTABLISHING BOUNDARIES AND HEALTHY COMMUNICATION

Establishing boundaries and practicing healthy communication are essential components of the forgiveness and letting go process within familial and intimate relationships. When hurt occurs, it is crucial to set clear boundaries that define what is acceptable and unacceptable behavior. This helps create a sense of safety and respect within the relationship.

Boundaries act as guidelines that protect our emotional well-being and ensure that our needs are met. They help establish a framework for healthy interaction and communication. By clearly communicating our boundaries to others, we can prevent further harm and foster an environment of mutual understanding and respect.

Healthy communication plays a vital role in the forgiveness and letting go process. It involves actively listening to one another, expressing thoughts and emotions honestly and respectfully, and practicing empathy and understanding. Effective communication allows for open dialogue, where both parties can share their perspectives, concerns, and desires.

When establishing boundaries and engaging in healthy communication, it is important to approach conversations with a willingness to understand and be understood. This involves actively listening without judgment, seeking clarification when needed, and expressing oneself in a calm and non-confrontational manner.

Setting boundaries and practicing healthy communication also requires recognizing and addressing patterns of unhealthy behavior. It may involve identifying and challenging negative communication styles such as defensiveness, blame, or criticism. Instead, focusing on constructive communication techniques like active listening, assertiveness, and empathy can foster understanding and promote healing.

Establishing boundaries and practicing healthy communication contribute to the process of forgiving and letting go by creating a foundation of trust, respect, and understanding. They provide a framework for resolving conflicts, addressing concerns, and working towards a healthier and more fulfilling relationship.

In conclusion, establishing boundaries and practicing healthy communication are integral to the forgiveness and letting go process within familial and intimate relationships. They help create an environment of respect, safety, and understanding. By setting clear boundaries and engaging in open and empathetic communication, individuals can foster healthier dynamics, resolve conflicts, and embark on a path of healing and growth.

9.3 LEARNING FROM THE EXPERIENCE AND GROWING STRONGER

Learning from the experience and growing stronger are essential aspects of the forgiveness and letting go process within familial and intimate relationships. When we encounter hurt and undergo the journey of forgiveness, it provides us with an opportunity for personal growth and transformation.

By reflecting on the experience, we can gain valuable insights into ourselves and our relationships. It allows us to examine our own actions and reactions, understand our vulnerabilities and triggers, and identify areas for personal development. Through this self-reflection, we can learn from our mistakes, take responsibility for our part in the situation, and make positive changes in our behavior.

Learning from the experience also involves gaining a deeper understanding of others. It allows us to recognize that everyone has their own struggles, vulnerabilities, and perspectives. By acknowledging the complexity of human nature, we can develop empathy and compassion towards the offender, which further supports the process of forgiveness.

Growing stronger through the forgiveness and letting go process involves building resilience and inner strength. It requires embracing the lessons learned, using them as a catalyst for personal growth, and developing a positive mindset. This may involve cultivating self-confidence, practicing self-care, and nurturing our emotional well-being.

Additionally, growing stronger entails cultivating a sense of gratitude and focusing on the positive aspects of life. It involves acknowledging the strength and resilience we have gained through the process of forgiveness and using it as a foundation for a brighter future. By embracing our growth and learning, we can let go of negative emotions and move forward with renewed strength and optimism.

It is important to remember that learning from the experience and growing stronger is a continuous process. Forgiveness and letting go are not one-time events but ongoing journeys. As we navigate through life and encounter new challenges, the lessons learned and the strength gained from previous experiences will continue to shape and empower us.

In conclusion, learning from the experience and growing stronger are integral to the forgiveness and letting go process within familial and intimate relationships. By reflecting on the situation, understanding ourselves and others, and using the experience as a catalyst for personal growth, we can emerge stronger and wiser. Embracing this growth allows us to move forward with resilience, optimism, and a deeper understanding of ourselves and those around us.

9.4 NURTURING A POSITIVE FUTURE

Nurturing a positive future is a crucial step in the process of moving forward and rebuilding trust within familial and intimate relationships. It involves creating a vision of the future that is filled with hope, love, and mutual growth.

To nurture a positive future, it is important to focus on the present moment and let go of past resentments and grudges. By embracing forgiveness and letting go, we free ourselves from the burden of carrying negative emotions that hinder our progress. Instead, we shift our energy towards creating a positive and harmonious environment where trust can flourish.

Building a positive future also requires setting clear intentions and goals for ourselves and our relationships. This involves identifying what we truly desire from our connections and actively working towards those aspirations. By envisioning a future that is aligned with our values and needs, we create a roadmap for growth and fulfillment.

Moreover, nurturing a positive future entails fostering open and honest communication. This means actively listening to one another, expressing ourselves authentically, and resolving conflicts in a constructive manner. By creating a safe and supportive space for dialogue, we cultivate understanding, empathy, and deeper connections.

In addition, it is essential to prioritize self-care and self-development. Taking care of our physical, mental, and emotional well-being allows us to show up fully in our relationships. This may involve engaging in activities that bring us joy, practicing self-compassion, and seeking personal growth opportunities. When we invest in ourselves, we enhance our capacity to contribute positively to our relationships and create a thriving future.

Furthermore, nurturing a positive future requires cultivating gratitude and appreciation. Taking time to acknowledge and celebrate the positive aspects of our relationships strengthens the bond between individuals. By expressing gratitude and showing appreciation for one another, we foster a positive atmosphere that nurtures trust, love, and mutual respect.

Lastly, it is important to remain adaptable and embrace change. Life is a journey filled with twists and turns, and relationships evolve over time. By being open to growth and embracing the unexpected, we can navigate challenges with resilience and optimism. Embracing change allows us to adapt, learn, and create new opportunities for a positive future.

In conclusion, nurturing a positive future is an integral part of moving forward and rebuilding trust within familial and intimate relationships. By letting go of the past, setting clear intentions, fostering open communication, prioritizing self-care, practicing gratitude, and embracing change, we create a foundation for a future that is filled with love, growth, and mutual well-being. It is through our collective efforts that we can create a positive future that strengthens our bonds and brings joy and fulfillment to our relationships.

9.5 CASE STUDY: EMMA, MICHAEL, AND LILY— REBUILDING TRUST IN A FAMILY

Emma, Michael, and Lily, a family faced significant challenges but managed to rebuild their trust and create a stronger bond.

Emma and Michael had been married for ten years when their relationship was deeply affected by a breach of trust. Emma had made a mistake that shattered Michael's trust and left him feeling betrayed. The incident had a profound impact on their marriage and their ability to connect emotionally.

With the support of a skilled therapist, Emma and Michael embarked on a journey of rebuilding trust. They recognized the importance of honesty, transparency, and open communication. Both individuals were committed to addressing their issues and working through their emotional pain.

Lily, their teenage daughter, also played a crucial role in the healing process. She felt the tension and sadness within the family and longed for a loving and trusting environment. Lily expressed her desire for a stronger connection with her parents and her willingness to participate actively in rebuilding trust.

Through therapy sessions and family discussions, Emma, Michael, and Lily began to establish new foundations for trust. They learned to listen to each other with empathy, express their emotions openly, and set clear boundaries to prevent future misunderstandings. Emma and Michael also engaged in individual healing work to address their own personal issues and to enhance their self-awareness.

Over time, their efforts paid off. Emma consistently demonstrated her remorse for her actions and took responsibility for rebuilding trust. Michael, in turn, gradually opened his heart to forgive and let go of the pain caused by the breach of trust. Lily witnessed her parents' commitment to healing and forgave them for their mistakes, strengthening the family bond further.

As the family continued their journey of moving forward and rebuilding trust, they experienced a profound transformation. Their communication deepened, allowing for vulnerability and understanding. They established healthy boundaries and learned to give each other space for personal growth. The foundation of trust was rebuilt, leading to a more harmonious and loving family dynamic.

The case study of Emma, Michael, and Lily demonstrates the resilience and dedication required to rebuild trust within a family. It highlights the significance of open communication, empathy, forgiveness, and personal growth. Through their journey, they inspire others to face challenges head-on, embrace healing, and rebuild trust, leading to stronger and more meaningful relationships within their families.

9.6 CONCLUSION

In conclusion, moving forward and rebuilding trust within familial and intimate relationships is a transformative journey that requires dedication, compassion, and a commitment to growth. By understanding the importance of rebuilding trust, establishing boundaries and healthy communication, learning from past experiences, and nurturing a positive future, we lay the groundwork for a renewed and flourishing connection. Through forgiveness, letting go, and intentional actions, we create the space for healing, growth, and the possibility of deepening our relationships in profound ways. As we embark on this path of healing and rebuilding, may we approach it with an open heart, resilience, and the belief that a brighter and more trusting future awaits us.

9.7 REFLECTIVE EXERCISE

Take a moment to reflect on a relationship where trust has been broken. Consider the impact of this breach of trust on both yourself and the relationship as a whole.

In your journal or on a separate piece of paper, write down the emotions and thoughts that arise as you think about rebuilding trust. Allow yourself to fully express your feelings without judgment or censorship.

Next, reflect on the steps you can take to rebuild trust in this relationship. Consider what boundaries need to be established, what communication practices can promote transparency and understanding, and what actions can demonstrate your commitment to rebuilding trust.

Write a letter to the person involved, expressing your intention to move forward and rebuild trust. Apologize for any role you may have played in the breakdown of trust, and outline the specific steps you are willing to take to rebuild it.

Reflect on the lessons learned from the experience. What insights or personal growth have you gained through this process? Write them down and consider how they can contribute to the positive evolution of the relationship.

Practice active listening and empathy as you engage in conversations with the person involved. Seek to understand their perspective, validate their feelings, and be open to feedback and constructive criticism.

Engage in activities together that foster trust and connection. This could involve participating in shared hobbies or interests, engaging in team-building exercises, or creating new positive memories together.

Regularly check in with yourself and the progress of the relationship. Reflect on any challenges or setbacks you may encounter, and seek support from a trusted friend or therapist if needed.

Celebrate milestones and successes in rebuilding trust. Acknowledge the progress made and express gratitude for the efforts put in by both parties.

Remember, rebuilding trust takes time and effort from all parties involved. Use these reflective exercises as tools to guide your journey of moving forward and rebuilding trust, and embrace the opportunity to create a stronger and more resilient relationship.

CHAPTER TEN

SUSTAINING FORGIVENESS AND LETTING GO

In this final chapter, we delve into the strategies and perspectives necessary to sustain forgiveness and the letting go process within familial and intimate relationships. As we navigate the complexities of life, it is crucial to develop tools and cultivate a mindset that supports the ongoing practice of forgiveness. By maintaining forgiveness in challenging times, coping with triggers and relapses, embracing the power of gratitude and mindfulness, and recognizing forgiveness as a lifelong practice, we pave the way for resilience, emotional well-being, and lasting harmony in our relationships.

10.1 MAINTAINING FORGIVENESS IN CHALLENGING TIMES

Forgiveness is a journey that requires ongoing effort and commitment, especially during challenging times. When faced with new difficulties or old wounds resurfacing, it can be tempting to revert to old patterns of resentment and anger. However, to sustain forgiveness within familial and intimate relationships, it is crucial to culti-vate a mindset of understanding and compassion.

During challenging times, it is important to remind ourselves of the reasons why we chose forgiveness in the first place. Reflect on the positive changes that forgive-ness has brought to your life and relationships. Remember that forgiveness is not a one-time event but an ongoing process. It requires us to consciously choose forgiveness each day, even when faced with adversity.

Another key aspect of maintaining forgiveness is prac-ticing self-awareness and self-care. Pay attention to your own emotions and reactions when faced with chal-lenging situations. Take time for self-reflection and identify any negative emotions that may be resurfacing. By acknowledging and understanding these emotions, you can consciously choose to respond with forgiveness and empathy rather than reacting with anger or resentment.

In challenging times, it can also be helpful to seek support from trusted friends, family, or even professional counselors. Share your struggles and concerns with them, and allow their guidance and perspective to provide you with strength and encouragement. Remember that you are not alone in this journey and that seeking support is a sign of strength, not weakness.

Additionally, practicing forgiveness during challenging times requires us to let go of the need for control and accept that we cannot change the past or others' behav-iors. Focus on what you can control, which is your own response and attitude towards the situation. By letting go of the need to control outcomes, you free yourself from the burden of carrying resentment and open up space for healing and growth.

Lastly, be patient with yourself and the process of forgiveness. It is natural to experience setbacks and moments of doubt. Remember that forgiveness is a choice that you can make each day. Celebrate your progress, no matter how small, and be gentle with yourself when facing challenges. Trust that as you continue to practice forgiveness in challenging times, you are nurturing a healthier and more harmonious future for yourself and your relationships.

In conclusion, sustaining forgiveness in challenging times requires dedication, self-awareness, and support. By maintaining a mindset of understanding and compassion, practicing self-care, seeking support, letting go of control, and being patient with yourself, you can navigate through difficult moments and sustain the transformative power of forgiveness in your familial and intimate relationships. Remember that forgiveness is not a destination but a lifelong journey of growth, healing, and love.

10.2 COPING WITH TRIGGERS AND RELAPSES

In the journey of forgiveness and letting go, it is common to encounter triggers and experience relapses, where old wounds resurface and bring back painful memories and emotions. Coping with these triggers and relapses is essential to sustain forgiveness within familial and intimate relationships.

Triggers can come in various forms—words, situations, or even certain individuals—that remind us of past hurts.

When faced with a trigger, it is important to practice self-awareness and recognize the emotions that arise. Allow yourself to acknowledge and validate these emotions without judgment. Understand that triggers do not define you or your progress in the forgiveness process.

One helpful strategy for coping with triggers is to develop a toolbox of healthy coping mechanisms. This can include deep breathing exercises, mindfulness techniques, engaging in physical activities, or writing in a journal. Experiment with different coping strategies and find what works best for you. When triggered, consciously choose to engage in these healthy coping mechanisms to redirect your focus and calm your mind.

Relapses, where you find yourself revisiting feelings of anger, resentment, or hurt, are also a common part of the forgiveness journey. It is crucial to approach relapses with self-compassion and understanding. Instead of berating yourself for slipping back into old patterns, use relapses as an opportunity for self-reflection and growth.

When experiencing a relapse, remind yourself that forgiveness is a process and setbacks are normal. Reflect on the progress you have made so far and the positive changes that forgiveness has brought into your life. Be patient with yourself and trust that you have the strength to overcome the relapse and continue moving forward on your journey of forgiveness.

In coping with triggers and relapses, it can be beneficial to seek support from loved ones or professional counselors. Share your experiences and struggles with trusted individuals who can provide guidance, empathy, and encouragement. Their support can remind you that you are not alone and that your journey towards forgiveness is valid and worthwhile.

Furthermore, practicing self-care is crucial in coping with triggers and relapses. Prioritize your emotional well-being by engaging in activities that bring you joy and peace. Nurture yourself with self-compassion, kindness, and forgiveness. Remember that you deserve healing and growth, and that setbacks are temporary.

Lastly, remind yourself of the bigger picture and the positive impact that forgiveness has on your relationships and overall well-being. Focus on the future and the potential for deeper connection, understanding, and peace. Embrace the opportunity to break free from the cycle of hurt and create a healthier and more harmonious environment for yourself and your loved ones.

In conclusion, coping with triggers and relapses is an important part of sustaining forgiveness in familial and intimate relationships. By practicing self-awareness, developing healthy coping mechanisms, approaching relapses with self-compassion, seeking support, prioritizing self-care, and focusing on the positive impact of forgiveness, you can navigate through triggers and relapses and continue on your journey of healing, growth, and lasting transformation. Remember, every step forward is a step towards greater emotional well-being and inner peace.

10.3 THE POWER OF GRATITUDE AND MINDFULNESS

In the pursuit of sustaining forgiveness and letting go within familial and intimate relationships, embracing the power of gratitude and mindfulness can greatly enhance our emotional well-being and deepen our connection with others. Gratitude and mindfulness are transformative practices that cultivate a positive and present mindset, allowing us to appreciate the beauty in our lives and nurture our relationships.

Gratitude is the practice of intentionally acknowledging and appreciating the blessings, big and small, that exist in our lives. It shifts our focus from what is lacking or hurtful to what we have and cherish. By cultivating gratitude, we open ourselves up to a sense of abundance and fulfillment, even in the face of challenges.

One way to incorporate gratitude into our daily lives is through the practice of keeping a gratitude journal. Each day, take a few moments to write down three things you are grateful for. They can be as simple as a sunny day, a kind word from a loved one, or a peaceful moment of solitude. By regularly reflecting on the things we appreciate, we train our minds to seek out the positive aspects of our experiences.

Mindfulness, on the other hand, is the practice of being fully present in the current moment, without judgment or attachment to the past or future. It allows us to cultivate a deep sense of awareness and acceptance of our thoughts, emotions, and sensations. Mindfulness helps us stay grounded and connected to the present, fostering clarity and compassion in our interactions with others.

Incorporating mindfulness into our lives can be as simple as taking a few mindful breaths throughout the day. Pause for a moment, bring your attention to your breath, and observe the sensations as you inhale and exhale. This simple act of mindfulness helps to anchor you in the present moment, allowing you to respond to situations with greater calmness and clarity.

By practicing gratitude and mindfulness together, we can deepen our appreciation for the present moment and the relationships we hold dear. When we approach forgiveness and letting go with a grateful heart and a mindful presence, we create space for compassion, understanding, and growth.

Gratitude and mindfulness also foster a sense of connection and empathy towards others. When we cultivate gratitude, we become more attuned to the kindness and support we receive from those around us. We recognize the efforts and intentions behind their actions, even if they have caused us pain in the past. This awareness opens the door to empathy and understanding, allowing us to see the humanity in others and nurture forgiveness within ourselves.

Moreover, mindfulness helps us become more aware of our own reactions and triggers, enabling us to respond to challenging situations with greater empathy and compassion. It reminds us to pause, reflect, and choose our words and actions mindfully, considering the impact they have on ourselves and others.

In conclusion, the power of gratitude and mindfulness cannot be underestimated in the journey of sustaining forgiveness and letting go within familial and intimate relationships. By cultivating gratitude, we shift our perspective to one of abundance and appreciation, allowing forgiveness to flourish. Through mindfulness, we develop a deep sense of presence and compassion, fostering understanding and growth. Embrace these practices as powerful tools on your path to lasting emotional well-being and harmonious relationships.

10.4 EMBRACING FORGIVENESS AS A LIFELONG PRACTICE

As we seal the final chapter of sustaining forgiveness and letting go within familial and intimate relationships, it is essential to recognize forgiveness as a lifelong practice rather than a one-time event. Forgiveness is not a destination to be reached but a continuous journey that requires commitment, self-reflection, and an open heart.

Embracing forgiveness as a lifelong practice means understanding that it is a process that unfolds over time. It involves acknowledging that healing and growth take time and effort. There may be setbacks, moments of doubt, and new challenges along the way, but it is through these experiences that we have the opportunity to deepen our understanding of forgiveness and ourselves.

One aspect of embracing forgiveness as a lifelong practice is the recognition that forgiveness is not a sign of weakness or surrender. Instead, it is an act of strength, courage, and compassion. It takes courage to let go of resentment, to release the grip of anger, and to open our hearts to healing. It is an act of self-empowerment to choose forgiveness and to free ourselves from the burdens of the past.

Another important aspect is the cultivation of self-awareness and self-reflection. Through self-reflection, we gain insights into our own patterns, triggers, and reactions. We can examine our own contributions to the challenges within our relationships and take responsibility for our actions. This self-awareness allows us to make conscious choices that align with our values and intentions, fostering forgiveness and healing.

Additionally, embracing forgiveness as a lifelong practice involves nurturing self-compassion and self-forgiveness. Just as we forgive others, we must extend the same forgiveness and understanding towards ourselves. We are all imperfect beings, capable of making mistakes and experiencing growth. By treating ourselves with kindness and compassion, we create a foundation of love and acceptance that supports our journey of forgiveness.

Forgiveness is not a linear process but a cyclical one. We may think we have forgiven completely, only to encounter new layers of pain or triggers that require further forgiveness and understanding. It is important to approach these moments with patience and grace, allowing ourselves the space and time to navigate through the emotions that arise.

Finally, embracing forgiveness as a lifelong practice means recognizing that forgiveness extends beyond our immediate relationships. It encompasses forgiveness towards ourselves, others, and even situations or circumstances. It is a mindset of letting go, releasing the attachment to past hurts, and embracing the present moment with a sense of openness and possibility.

In conclusion, embracing forgiveness as a lifelong practice is an invitation to engage in an ongoing journey of growth, healing, and emotional liberation. It requires commitment, self-reflection, and self-compassion. By recognizing forgiveness as a continuous process, we create the opportunity for deep transformation within ourselves and our relationships. As we navigate the complexities of life, let us embrace forgiveness as a guiding principle, allowing it to shape our actions, nurture our well-being, and cultivate lasting harmony in our familial and intimate connections.

10.5 CASE STUDY: BENJAMIN—SUSTAINING FORGIVENESS AND LETTING GO

Let's consider the story of Benjamin, an extraordinary man who embraced the practice of forgiveness and actively nurtured the art of letting go.

Benjamin had faced deep emotional wounds and betrayals in his past. The weight of resentment and pain burdened him for years, causing turmoil in his life and relationships. Determined to find solace and move forward, Benjamin committed himself to the process of forgiveness and the ongoing practice of releasing attachments.

Benjamin understood that sustaining forgiveness required resilience and an unwavering commitment. He embraced forgiveness as an integral part of his life, knowing that it demanded continuous effort and introspection. Benjamin recognized that there might be challenging moments when past hurts resurfaced, but he remained steadfast in his dedication to freeing himself from their grip.

Benjamin developed a repertoire of strategies to sustain forgiveness and embrace the art of letting go. He nurtured self-compassion, offering himself kindness and understanding when confronted with triggers or moments of vulnerability. Benjamin also cultivated mindfulness, immersing himself in the present moment and observing his thoughts and emotions with non-judgmental awareness.

During his path, Benjamin encountered instances of relapse, where anger or resentment attempted to reclaim its hold. However, he steadfastly reminded himself of the healing power of forgiveness and the liberation that accompanies letting go. Benjamin engaged in self-reflection, seeking solace in trusted friends and a therapist who provided guidance and support. Their encouragement and wisdom aided him in navigating through trying times, reinforcing his commitment to the forgiveness journey.

Moreover, Benjamin recognized the potency of gratitude in sustaining forgiveness. He practiced gratitude daily, focusing on the blessings in his life and acknowledging the personal growth he had attained through forgiveness. This practice nurtured a positive mindset and fortified his determination to release the past's grip.

As Benjamin continued on his path, he experienced a remarkable transformation. The burdens of resentment and anger gradually dissipated, allowing him to embrace a newfound sense of freedom and inner peace. Benjamin's relationships flourished as well, as he approached them with enhanced compassion, understanding, and empathy.

Benjamin's story serves as a powerful testament for those seeking to sustain forgiveness and liberate themselves from the past's chains. Through his unwavering dedication, resilience, and commitment to personal growth, he exemplifies the possibility of breaking free from the clutches of resentment and discovering inner peace. Benjamin's narrative reminds us that forgiveness is an ongoing practice, and by embracing it, we can foster emotional well-being, strengthen our relationships, and cultivate a more fulfilling life.

10.6 CONCLUSION

In this final chapter, we have explored the strategies and perspectives needed to sustain forgiveness and the letting go process within familial and intimate relationships. We have seen the importance of maintaining forgiveness in challenging times, coping with triggers and relapses, embracing gratitude and mindfulness, and recognizing forgiveness as a lifelong practice. By integrating these principles into our lives, we have the power to cultivate resilience, deepen our emotional well-being, and foster lasting harmony in our relationships. As we embark on the journey of sustaining forgiveness and letting go, let us carry with us the understanding that forgiveness is not a destination but a continuous process of growth and transformation. Through our commitment to forgiveness, we can create a future filled with love, compassion, and genuine connection.

10.7 REFLECTIVE EXERCISE

Take a moment to reflect on the journey of forgiveness and letting go that you have embarked upon. Consider the challenges you have faced and the progress you have made thus far.

In your journal or on a separate piece of paper, write down the moments when you have been able to sustain forgiveness. Reflect on the strategies and perspectives that have supported you in maintaining forgiveness, even in difficult circumstances.

Think about the triggers or situations that tend to test your ability to sustain forgiveness. Write them down and explore ways to proactively cope with these triggers. Consider techniques such as deep breathing, grounding exercises, or engaging in activities that bring you joy and peace.

Practice gratitude and mindfulness as tools for sustaining forgiveness. Each day, write down three things you are grateful for related to your journey of forgiveness. Cultivate a sense of appreciation for the lessons learned, the growth experienced, and the healing that has taken place.

Consider forgiveness as a lifelong practice rather than a one-time event. Reflect on how forgiveness can be integrated into your daily life and relationships. Explore ways to nurture forgiveness through self-compassion, empathy, and open-heartedness.

Engage in regular self-reflection to assess your progress in sustaining forgiveness. Ask yourself questions such as:

How has forgiveness impacted my overall well-being? What areas still require my attention and compassion? What can I do to continue cultivating forgiveness in my life?

Share your journey with a trusted friend, therapist, or support group. Discuss the challenges and successes you have experienced in sustaining forgiveness. Seek guidance and encouragement from those who understand the transformative power of forgiveness.

Create a personal mantra or affirmation related to forgiveness that you can repeat to yourself during challenging moments. For example, "I choose forgiveness and release for my own peace and growth."

Celebrate your accomplishments in sustaining forgiveness. Acknowledge the strength and resilience you have demonstrated throughout your journey. Treat yourself with kindness and self-care as you continue to embrace the path of forgiveness and letting go.

Remember, sustaining forgiveness is an ongoing process that requires dedication and self-awareness. Use these reflective exercises as tools to support your ongoing practice of forgiveness, and embrace the profound impact it can have on your relationships and overall well-being.

AFTERWORD

In this comprehensive exploration of forgiveness and letting go within familial and intimate relationships, we have delved into the depths of healing, growth, and transformation. We have discovered that forgiveness is a complex and multifaceted journey, requiring courage, vulnerability, and resilience. Throughout each chapter, we have examined the importance of acknowledging pain, shifting perspectives, releasing resentment and anger, cultivating empathy and understanding, practicing self-forgiveness, and the art of letting go.

Through this journey, we have learned that forgiveness is not a one-time event, but a continuous process that requires patience, self-reflection, and a commitment to personal and relational well-being. It is a powerful tool that has the potential to heal deep wounds, restore trust, and create space for new beginnings. By embracing forgiveness, we not only free ourselves from the burdens of the past but also pave the way for healthier, more fulfilling relationships.

However, it is essential to acknowledge that forgiveness does not mean forgetting or condoning the harm caused. It is a choice to release the grip of resentment and choose a path of healing and growth. Forgiveness does not always come easily, and it may require time, support, and self-compassion. It is a process that varies for each individual and relationship, and there is no one-size-fits-all approach.

As we conclude this journey, let us remember that forgiveness is a gift we give ourselves. It is a courageous act of self-love and liberation from the shackles of pain. It is a choice to embrace our humanity, acknowledge our own imperfections, and extend grace to ourselves and others. By fostering forgiveness in our lives, we create a ripple effect that extends beyond our immediate relationships, contributing to a more compassionate and harmonious world.

May this exploration serve as a guide and inspiration as you embark on your own forgiveness and letting go journey. May you find the strength to release the past, embrace the present, and create a future filled with love, understanding, and connection. May forgiveness be your path to personal healing, relationship renewal, and inner peace.

RECAP OF THE FORGIVENESS PROCESS

Throughout this book, we have explored the process of forgiveness within familial and intimate relationships. Let's recap the key steps we've discussed:

Firstly, we acknowledged the pain caused by the offense, allowing ourselves to understand its impact and importance.

Next, we shifted perspectives by examining the situation from different angles, practicing empathy, and recognizing the humanity of the offender. This helped us gain new insights and possibilities for healing.

We then focused on releasing resentment and anger, understanding their destructive nature, and learning techniques to manage and channel these emotions in healthy ways.

Cultivating empathy and understanding became crucial as we emphasized active listening, open communication, and seeking to understand the offender's perspective.

We explored the significance of self-forgiveness, letting go of guilt and shame, and embracing imperfection and personal growth.

The art of letting go involved detaching emotionally from the past, releasing attachments to the offense and offender, and creating symbolic acts to symbolize letting go.

Rebuilding trust became a priority, as we established boundaries, practiced healthy communication, learned from the experience, and nurtured a positive future.

Lastly, we discussed sustaining forgiveness and letting go. This involved maintaining forgiveness during challenging times, coping with triggers and relapses, embracing gratitude and mindfulness, and recognizing forgiveness as a lifelong practice.

Throughout this journey, we learned that forgiveness is a continuous process that requires patience, self-reflection, and a commitment to personal and relational well-being. It is an act of self-love and liberation from the burdens of the past.

Remember, forgiveness does not mean forgetting or condoning the harm caused. It is a choice to release resentment and choose a path of healing and growth. Each individual and relationship may have their own unique forgiveness process.

By embracing forgiveness, we free ourselves from the chains of pain, restore trust, and create space for new beginnings. It is a gift we give ourselves, extending grace and compassion to both ourselves and others.

As you continue your own forgiveness journey, may you find the strength and courage to let go of the past, embrace the present, and create a future filled with love, understanding, and connection. May forgiveness be your path to personal healing, relationship renewal, and inner peace.

REFLECTION EXERCISES

Journaling Prompts

1. Reflect on a past hurtful experience within a familial or intimate relationship. Write about how it has impacted you emotionally, mentally, and spiritually.
2. Describe your current relationship with forgiveness. What beliefs, attitudes, or barriers do you have towards forgiveness?
3. Explore your understanding of letting go. What does it mean to you, and what challenges do you anticipate in the process?
4. Identify any recurring patterns or themes in your relationships that may hinder forgiveness and letting go. Reflect on their origins and potential influences.

Self-Reflection Questions

1. How does holding onto resentment and anger affect your overall well-being and relationships?
2. In what ways have past hurts shaped your perception of yourself and your ability to trust others?
3. Consider a specific person you struggle to forgive. What emotions arise when you think about them? What do you hope to gain from forgiving them?
4. Reflect on moments when you have received forgiveness from others. How did it make you feel, and what impact did it have on your relationship with the person who forgave you?

Visualization Exercise

Close your eyes and imagine yourself releasing a symbolic object that represents the pain and resentment you carry. Visualize it floating away, freeing you from its weight. How does this act of letting go make you feel? What changes do you envision in your life as a result?

Gratitude Practice

Take a moment to write down three things you are grateful for in your relationships, despite the challenges and hurts you have experienced. Reflect on how cultivating gratitude can shift your perspective and contribute to forgiveness and letting go.

Future Visioning

1. Envision a future where forgiveness and letting go have taken place. Describe the ideal state of

your relationships and the impact it has on your overall well-being.

2. Identify specific actions or behaviors you can engage in to foster forgiveness and create a positive environment within your relationships.

Forgiveness Letter

Write a forgiveness letter addressed to yourself, expressing compassion and understanding for any perceived shortcomings or mistakes you have made in your relationships. Embrace forgiveness as an act of self-compassion and extend forgiveness to yourself for any self-blame or guilt you may be holding onto.

Empathy Exercise

Choose a person who has hurt you and put yourself in their shoes. Reflect on their life experiences, challenges, and personal struggles that may have contributed to their actions. How does practicing empathy towards them affect your perspective on forgiveness?

Release Ritual

Create a personal ritual to symbolize the act of letting go. It can be lighting a candle and blowing it out, tearing up a written representation of your pain, or any other symbolic gesture that resonates with you. Engage in this ritual with the intention of releasing negative emotions and making space for healing and growth.

Healing Visualization

Close your eyes and imagine a healing light enveloping the wounds caused by past hurts. Visualize this light gradually soothing and healing those areas, bringing a sense of peace and restoration. Notice how this visualization affects your emotional state and overall well-being.

Gratitude Letter

Write a gratitude letter to someone who has played a significant role in your forgiveness journey. Express your appreciation for their support, understanding, or act of forgiveness. Share how their presence or actions have impacted your life and contributed to your healing process.

Remember, reflection exercises are deeply personal, and it is important to approach them at your own pace and comfort level. They serve as tools for self-discovery and self-reflection, allowing you to delve into your emotions, beliefs, and experiences surrounding forgiveness and letting go. Take the time to engage with these exercises mindfully, and be gentle with yourself as you navigate the path towards healing and growth.

GUIDED MEDITATIONS

Guided Meditation 1: Cultivating Forgiveness

Begin by finding a comfortable position, either sitting or lying down. Close your eyes and take a deep breath in, allowing your body to relax with each exhale.

1. Bring to mind a situation or person that you are seeking forgiveness for. Visualize their presence in front of you, and imagine yourself surrounded by a warm, loving light.

2. Repeat the following affirmation silently or out loud: "I am open to forgiving and releasing any feelings of anger, resentment, or hurt. I choose forgiveness for my own well-being."

3. Take a moment to reflect on the pain that this situation or person has caused you. Acknowledge the emotions that arise, allowing them to be present without judgment.

4. Visualize a river flowing beside you. As you imagine this river, see your pain and hurt transformed into a small boat or leaf floating gently on the water's surface.

5. Watch as the boat or leaf slowly drifts away, carried downstream by the gentle current. Allow yourself to feel a sense of relief and lightness as you let go of the burdens of the past.

6. Take a deep breath in, and as you exhale, imagine releasing any remaining negative emotions. Feel a sense of forgiveness and compassion filling your heart, freeing you from the weight of resentment.

7. Repeat the affirmation: "I forgive myself and others. I release the past and embrace a future of peace and healing."

8. Take a few moments to sit in stillness, focusing on your breath and the sensation of peace within. When you are ready, gently open your eyes and carry this feeling of forgiveness and letting go with you throughout your day.

Guided Meditation 2: Letting Go of Attachments

Find a quiet and comfortable space where you can sit or lie down. Close your eyes and take a few deep breaths, allowing yourself to relax.

1. Bring your attention to the present moment. Notice any physical sensations in your body and the rhythm of your breath.
2. Visualize yourself in a peaceful garden or natural setting. Imagine the beauty of this place, with vibrant flowers, flowing water, and gentle breezes.
3. Begin to reflect on any attachments or expectations you may have towards yourself or others. Notice the thoughts, emotions, or memories that arise as you explore these attachments.
4. Imagine these attachments as strings or ropes tied around your body and mind, creating a sense of tension and restriction.
5. With each exhale, imagine loosening these ropes and releasing the attachments. Visualize them falling away, allowing you to experience a sense of lightness and freedom.
6. As you let go, repeat the affirmation: "I release all attachments that no longer serve me. I embrace the present moment with acceptance and gratitude."
7. Focus on your breath and the sensation of openness in your body and mind. Allow yourself to fully experience the present moment, free from the constraints of attachments.

8. Take a moment to express gratitude for this practice of letting go and the opportunities it brings for growth and transformation.

9. When you are ready, gently bring your awareness back to the room, wiggle your fingers and toes, and slowly open your eyes. Carry this sense of release and openness with you as you navigate your day.

Guided Meditation 3: Cultivating Self-Compassion

Find a quiet and comfortable space where you can sit or lie down. Close your eyes and take a few deep breaths, allowing your body to relax.

1. Begin by bringing your attention to your heart center. Place your hand gently over your heart and feel its gentle rise and fall with each breath.

2. Take a moment to acknowledge any feelings of self-judgment or criticism that may be present. Allow yourself to fully recognize these emotions without judgment.

3. With each inhale, imagine breathing in love, compassion, and acceptance. Feel these qualities filling your heart space and radiating throughout your entire being.

4. As you exhale, release any self-judgment, criticism, or negative self-talk. Imagine these thoughts dissipating like clouds in the sky, leaving behind a clear and peaceful state of mind.

5. Repeat the following affirmations silently or out loud: "I am worthy of love and forgiveness. I

embrace my imperfections with compassion and kindness."

6. Visualize a soft, warm light surrounding your entire body, enveloping you in a cocoon of self-compassion. Feel this light bringing healing and comfort to any wounded parts of yourself.

7. Take a few moments to reflect on moments of self-forgiveness and self-acceptance in your life. Recall times when you showed yourself kindness and understanding.

8. Imagine extending forgiveness and compassion to yourself for any past mistakes or shortcomings. See yourself letting go of any guilt or shame, and embracing a deep sense of self-love.

9. Breathe in deeply, allowing this self-compassion and forgiveness to fill every cell of your being. As you exhale, release any remaining tension or resistance, surrendering to the flow of self-love.

10. Take a few moments to simply be present with yourself, bathing in the warmth and healing energy of self-compassion. Allow this practice to nourish and uplift you.

11. When you are ready, gently bring your awareness back to the room. Wiggle your fingers and toes, and slowly open your eyes. Carry this sense of self-compassion and forgiveness with you, knowing that it is always available to support and nurture you.

Guided Meditation 4: Cultivating Gratitude and Letting Go

Find a comfortable and quiet space where you can sit or lie down. Close your eyes and take a few deep breaths, allowing yourself to relax and become present in the moment.

1. Begin by focusing your attention on your breath. Notice the sensation of the breath entering and leaving your body. Allow each breath to help you deepen your sense of relaxation and calm.

2. Bring to mind something or someone that you are grateful for in your life. It could be a person, a situation, a quality within yourself, or anything that brings you a sense of joy and appreciation.

3. As you think about this person or thing, allow yourself to fully experience the gratitude and appreciation you have for it. Notice how it feels in your body and the positive emotions it brings forth.

4. Now, shift your focus to something that you are holding onto that no longer serves you. It could be a past hurt, a grudge, or a negative belief about yourself or others. Acknowledge its presence without judgment.

5. As you continue to breathe deeply, imagine that with each exhale, you are releasing and letting go of this negative energy or emotion. Visualize it leaving your body and dissipating into the air, allowing space for new positive energy to enter.

6. As you let go, affirm to yourself, "I release what no longer serves me. I am open to forgiveness and healing."

7. Bring your attention back to the feeling of gratitude. Allow it to expand within you, filling

    your heart and radiating throughout your entire being.

8. Take a few moments to reflect on the ways in which gratitude can support your journey of forgiveness and letting go. Consider how it can shift your perspective, invite compassion, and cultivate a sense of peace within.

9. Embrace a deep sense of gratitude for the lessons you have learned from past experiences. Recognize that even the most challenging situations can be catalysts for growth and transformation.

10. Sit with the feelings of gratitude and the sense of letting go. Allow them to coexist within you, knowing that you have the power to choose which emotions you nurture and cultivate.

11. When you are ready, gently bring your awareness back to the present moment. Wiggle your fingers and toes, and slowly open your eyes. Carry the sense of gratitude and the willingness to let go with you as you continue on your journey.

Remember, forgiveness and letting go are personal processes, and cultivating gratitude can be a powerful tool to support them. Use this guided meditation as a way to anchor yourself in gratitude and release what no longer serves you.

FORGIVENESS WORKSHEETS

Instructions: Take some time to reflect on the offense or hurt that you have experienced. Use this worksheet to explore your thoughts, emotions, and the impact it has had on you.

FORGIVENESS WORKSHEET 1: REFLECTING ON THE OFFENSE

1. Describe the offense or hurt in detail.

2. How has this offense impacted your life?

3. What emotions arise when you think about the offense?

4. Reflect on how this offense has influenced your thoughts and beliefs.

5. Consider any patterns or behaviors that have emerged.

6. Write down any resentments or grudges you may be holding onto.

7. Reflect on the consequences of holding onto this offense.

8. Are there any lessons or insights you have gained from this experience?

FORGIVENESS WORKSHEET 2: SHIFTING PERSPECTIVES AND EMPATHY

1. Put yourself in the offender's shoes.

2. Consider any personal struggles or challenges the offender may be facing.

3. Reflect on any external factors or circumstances that may have influenced the situation.

4. Explore the possibility of forgiveness as a way to break the cycle of hurt.

FORGIVENESS WORKSHEET 3: LETTING GO AND SELF-FORGIVENESS

1. Identify any feelings of guilt or shame related to the offense.

2. Reflect on why you may be struggling to let go.

3. Explore the concept of self-forgiveness.

4. Write a letter to yourself expressing forgiveness and compassion.

5. Consider actions to nurture self-forgiveness and promote healing and growth.

WORKSHEET 4: REBUILDING TRUST AND ESTABLISHING BOUNDARIES

1. Reflect on the importance of rebuilding trust in your relationship.

2. Identify any specific boundaries you need to establish for your well-being.

3. Consider effective communication strategies for expressing your boundaries.

4. Reflect on any fears or concerns you may have about rebuilding trust.

5. Identify actions you can take to rebuild trust and strengthen your connection.

WORKSHEET 5: CULTIVATING EMPATHY AND UNDERSTANDING

1. Reflect on the importance of empathy and understanding in relationships.

2. Consider any barriers that may prevent you from empathizing with others.

3. Explore techniques for practicing active listening and open communication.

4. Reflect on ways you can seek to understand others' perspectives.

5. Identify common ground and shared values to foster empathy and understanding.

Worksheet 6: Sustaining Forgiveness and Letting Go

1. Reflect on the challenges of sustaining forgiveness in difficult times.

2. Identify triggers that may cause relapses in your forgiveness journey.

3. Explore the power of gratitude and mindfulness in sustaining forgiveness.

4. Consider forgiveness as a lifelong practice and embrace its ongoing nature.

5. Reflect on ways you can nurture forgiveness and let go on a daily basis.

SUPPORTIVE ORGANIZATIONS

Here is a list of organizations and support networks that specialize in forgiveness, relationship counseling, and emotional well-being. These organizations can provide professional guidance, therapy, and community resources to support you on your journey of healing and rebuilding relationships:

1. American Association for Marriage and Family Therapy (AAMFT) - A professional organization that provides resources and information on marriage and family therapy, including finding therapists in your area.
2. National Association of Relationship and Marriage Educators (NARME) - An organization that promotes healthy relationships through education and support, offering resources and workshops for couples and individuals.
3. International Forgiveness Institute - A nonprofit organization dedicated to promoting forgiveness education and research, providing resources, workshops, and support for individuals seeking to cultivate forgiveness in their lives.
4. The Gottman Institute - Founded by renowned relationship experts Drs. John and Julie Gottman, this institute offers resources, workshops, and therapy to help couples build and maintain healthy relationships.
5. National Domestic Violence Hotline - A 24/7 hotline providing support, information, and resources for individuals experiencing domestic violence or abuse. They can offer guidance on

safety planning and connecting with local support services.

6. Mental Health America - A leading mental health organization that provides information, resources, and support for individuals seeking help for various mental health concerns, including relationship issues.

7. The American Psychological Association (APA) - A professional organization that offers resources, publications, and referrals to psychologists specializing in relationship counseling and emotional well-being.

8. National Alliance on Mental Illness (NAMI) - A grassroots mental health organization providing education, support, and advocacy for individuals and families affected by mental health conditions. They offer resources and referrals for therapy and support groups.

9. National Suicide Prevention Lifeline - A 24/7 hotline providing support and crisis intervention for individuals in emotional distress or experiencing suicidal thoughts. They can help connect individuals to local mental health resources.

10. Your local community centers, counseling centers, or religious organizations may also offer counseling services, support groups, and workshops focused on forgiveness, relationship counseling, and emotional well-being. Check your local directory or online resources for more information.

Remember, seeking support from qualified professionals and organizations can greatly assist you in your journey towards forgiveness, healing, and building healthier relationships.

RECOMMENDED PAPERS

Here are some recommended published papers that explore the topic of forgiveness and letting go:

1. Exline, J. J., Baumeister, R. F., Bushman, B. J., Campbell, W. K., & Finkel, E. J. (2004). Too Proud to Let Go: Narcissistic Entitlement as a Barrier to Forgiveness. *Journal of Personality and Social Psychology*, 87(6), 894-912.

2. McCullough, M. E., Bellah, C. G., Kilpatrick, S. D., & Johnson, J. L. (2001). Vengefulness: Relationships with Forgiveness, Rumination, Well-Being, and the Big Five. *Personality and Social Psychology Bulletin*, 27(5), 601-610.

3. Strelan, P., & Covic, T. (2006). A Review of Forgiveness Process Models and a Coping Framework to Guide Future Research. *Journal of Social and Clinical Psychology*, 25(10), 1059-1085.

4. Toussaint, L. L., Williams, D. R., Musick, M. A., & Everson, S. A. (2001). Forgiveness and health: Age Differences in a US Probability Sample. *Journal of Adult Development*, 8(4), 249-257.

5. Worthington, E. L., Witvliet, C. V. O., Pietrini, P., & Miller, A. J. (2007). Forgiveness, Health, And Well-Being: A Review of Evidence for Emotional versus Decisional Forgiveness, Dispositional

Forgivingness, and Reduced Unforgiveness. *Journal of Behavioral Medicine*, 30(4), 291-302.

These papers offer valuable insights into the psychological, emotional, and health-related aspects of forgiveness and letting go. They provide a foundation for understanding the research and theories behind forgiveness and its impact on well-being. Reading these papers can enhance your knowledge and deepen your understanding of forgiveness from a scientific perspective.